First World War
and Army of Occupation
War Diary
France, Belgium and Germany

19 DIVISION
Divisional Troops
87 Brigade Royal Field Artillery
17 July 1915 - 31 October 1918

WO95/2067/4

The Naval & Military Press Ltd
www.nmarchive.com
Published in association with The National Archives

Published by

The Naval & Military Press Ltd

Unit 10 Ridgewood Industrial Park,

Uckfield, East Sussex,

TN22 5QE England

Tel: +44 (0) 1825 749494

www.naval-military-press.com

www.nmarchive.com

This diary has been reprinted in facsimile from the original. Any imperfections are inevitably reproduced and the quality may fall short of modern type and cartographic standards.

© Crown Copyright
Images reproduced by permission of The National Archives, London, England, 2015.

Contents

Document type	Place/Title	Date From	Date To
Heading	19 Div-87 Bde R.F.A. Jul 1915-Oct 1918		
Heading	19th Division 87th Brigade R.F.A. Jly 1915-Oct 1918		
Heading	19th Division 87th Brigade R.F.A. Vol I Jly & Aug 15		
War Diary	Bulford	17/07/1915	18/07/1915
War Diary	Havre	19/07/1915	19/07/1915
War Diary	Ruminghem	20/07/1915	23/08/1915
War Diary	Renescure	24/07/1915	24/07/1915
War Diary	Ham-En-Artois	24/07/1915	01/08/1915
War Diary	Chlle Duvelle	01/08/1915	24/08/1915
War Diary	Loisne	25/08/1915	31/08/1915
Miscellaneous	I Reportion Operations Of The Days		
Miscellaneous	I Tactical Progress Report		
Miscellaneous	Tactical Progress Report I Report On Operations Of The Day	31/08/1915	31/08/1915
War Diary	Loisne	01/09/1915	30/09/1915
Miscellaneous	Tactical Progress Report I Report on operations of the day	01/09/1915	01/09/1915
Miscellaneous	Tactical Progress Report I Report on Operations of the day	02/09/1915	02/09/1915
Miscellaneous	Tactical Progress Report I Report on operations of the day		
Miscellaneous	Tactical Progress Report I Report on operations of the day	04/09/1915	04/09/1915
Miscellaneous	Tactical Progress Report I Report on operations of the day	06/09/1915	06/09/1915
Miscellaneous	13		
Miscellaneous	Tactical Progress Report I Report on operations of the day	07/09/1915	07/09/1915
Miscellaneous	14		
Miscellaneous	Tactical Progress Report I Report on operations of the day	08/09/1915	08/09/1915
Miscellaneous	15		
Miscellaneous	Tactical Progress Report I Report On Operation Of The Day	09/09/1915	09/09/1915
Miscellaneous	Tactical Progress Report I Report On Operation Of The Day	10/09/1915	10/09/1915
Miscellaneous	16		
Miscellaneous	Tactical Progress Report I Report On Operations Of The Day	12/09/1915	12/09/1915
Miscellaneous	17		
Miscellaneous	Tactical Progress Report I Report On Operations Of The Day	13/09/1915	13/09/1915
Miscellaneous	Tactical Progress Report I Report On Operation Of The Day	15/09/1915	15/09/1915
Miscellaneous	19		
Miscellaneous	Firing Report from O.C. C/87th BM to O.C. 87th. BM R.F.A. from 9.0 am 15/9/15 to 9.0 am 16/9/15		
Miscellaneous	Tactical Progress Report	16/09/1915	16/09/1915
Miscellaneous	Tactical Progress Report		

Miscellaneous	Tactical Progress Report I Report On Operation Of The Day	17/09/1915	17/09/1915
Miscellaneous	21		
Miscellaneous	Firing Report from O.C. C/87th BM to O.C. 87th BM R.F.A. from 9.0 am 17/9/15 to 9.0 am 18/9/15		
Miscellaneous	Tactical Progress Report		
Miscellaneous	Tactical Progress Report I Report on operations of the day	18/09/1915	18/09/1915
Miscellaneous	22		
Miscellaneous	Tactical Progress		
Miscellaneous	Tactical Progress Report I Report On Operation Of The Day	21/09/1915	21/09/1915
Miscellaneous	25		
Miscellaneous	Tactical Progress Report I Report on operations of the day	19/09/1915	19/09/1915
Miscellaneous	23		
Miscellaneous	Tactical Progress Report I Report on operations of the day	20/09/1915	20/09/1915
Miscellaneous	24		
Heading	19th Division 87th Bde R.F.A. Vol 3 Oct 15		
War Diary	Loisne	01/10/1915	07/10/1915
War Diary	Rue Des Vaches	07/10/1915	15/10/1915
War Diary	Q14a 610	15/10/1915	21/10/1915
War Diary	Loisne	21/10/1915	31/10/1915
Heading	19th Division 87th Bde R.F.A. Vol 4 Nov 15		
War Diary	Loisne	01/11/1915	27/11/1915
War Diary		24/11/1915	24/11/1915
Heading	19th Div Dec 1915 87th Bde: R.F.A. Vol 5 Dec 1915		
War Diary	St Venant	01/12/1915	04/12/1915
War Diary	Bout De Ville	05/12/1915	31/12/1915
Heading	87th Bde. R.F.A. Vol: 6		
War Diary	Bout De Ville	01/01/1916	30/01/1916
War Diary	Haverskque	31/01/1916	31/01/1916
War Diary	Croix Marraisse	01/02/1916	18/03/1916
War Diary	Lacouture	25/03/1916	16/04/1916
War Diary	Haverskerque	17/04/1916	21/04/1916
War Diary	Therouanne	23/04/1916	30/04/1916
Miscellaneous	J.D. 164. To A.Gs. Office at the Base	08/06/1916	08/06/1916
Miscellaneous	87th. F. A. Brigade. Nominal Roll Of Officers W. Os. N. C. Cs. & Men.	07/06/1916	07/06/1916
Miscellaneous	Nominal Roll of Officer. W.Os. N. COs men of A/87. F.A. Bde.		
Miscellaneous	B/87th Brigade R.F.A.		
Miscellaneous	C/87 Bde. R.F.A. nominal Roll of officers Warrant Officers, N.C.O's. & men	07/06/1916	07/06/1916
Miscellaneous	Nominal Roll Of Officers W.Os. N.C.O. & Men D/87th F.A. Bde.	07/06/1916	07/06/1916
Miscellaneous	Nominal Roll-W/19 Hy. T.M. Battery	07/06/1916	07/06/1916
War Diary	Therouanne	01/05/1916	06/05/1916
War Diary	Belloy-Sur-Somme	07/05/1916	31/05/1916
War Diary	Belloy-Sur-Somme	01/06/1916	20/06/1916
War Diary	Buire	20/06/1916	29/06/1916
War Diary	Tara	30/06/1916	30/06/1916
Heading	Headquarters 87th Brigade R.F.A. July 1916		
War Diary	Tara	01/07/1916	20/07/1916
War Diary	Tara Redoubt	20/07/1916	20/07/1916

War Diary	Tara	20/07/1916	21/07/1916
War Diary	Mrl Boro Wood	22/07/1916	31/07/1916
Heading	87th Brigade Royal Field Artillery August 1916		
War Diary	Marlboro Wood	01/08/1916	04/08/1916
War Diary	Becourt	05/08/1916	05/08/1916
War Diary	Beaucourt Saleux	06/08/1916	07/08/1916
War Diary	Steenvoorde	08/08/1916	08/08/1916
War Diary	Kemmel Shelters	09/08/1916	31/08/1916
War Diary	Kemmel	01/09/1916	08/09/1916
War Diary	Kemmel T23 C 42	09/09/1916	16/09/1916
War Diary	T23 C 4 2	17/09/1916	30/09/1916
War Diary	Ploegsteerte	01/10/1916	16/10/1916
War Diary	Constance Trench	16/10/1916	17/11/1916
War Diary	X. 2 B. 2.9	22/11/1916	30/11/1916
War Diary		01/12/1916	25/12/1916
War Diary	Sarton Colincamp	02/01/1917	02/01/1917
War Diary	Sailly-Au-Bois	15/01/1917	31/01/1917
War Diary		01/02/1916	27/02/1916
War Diary		01/03/1917	31/03/1917
War Diary		01/04/1917	30/04/1917
War Diary	Ypres	01/05/1917	10/05/1917
War Diary	Kleine Vierstraat Farm	11/05/1917	30/05/1917
War Diary		13/05/1917	31/05/1917
War Diary	Kleine Vierstraat Farm	01/06/1917	30/06/1917
War Diary	HQrs 87th R.F. A.B. at N 17 C 34	01/07/1917	31/07/1917
War Diary	N 17c 3.4 (Nr Wytschaete)	01/08/1917	10/08/1917
War Diary	X17b 6.6 (Nr Bailleul)	11/08/1917	21/08/1917
War Diary	Strazeele	24/08/1917	31/08/1917
War Diary	Strazeele	01/09/1917	05/09/1917
War Diary	Ref Sheet 28 N W 1/20,000	06/09/1917	27/09/1917
Miscellaneous	19th Division "A"	07/11/1917	07/11/1917
War Diary	N 10 B 9.4 (Sheet 28)	01/11/1917	29/11/1917
War Diary	Locre	01/11/1917	30/11/1917
War Diary	Bedford House (Nr Ypres)	01/12/1917	31/12/1917
War Diary	Etricourt	01/01/1918	02/01/1918
War Diary	Neuville	03/01/1918	08/01/1918
War Diary	Hindenburg Support	08/01/1918	31/01/1918
War Diary	Q12 A 2.5 (Sheet 57c 1/40.000	01/02/1918	15/02/1918
War Diary	Neuville & Ytres	16/02/1918	28/02/1918
Heading	This Diary Is Party Mutilated. 87th Brigade Royal Field Artillery March 1918		
War Diary	Neuville Bourjonval	01/03/1918	22/03/1918
War Diary	Le Mesnil	23/03/1918	23/03/1918
War Diary	Le Sars	24/03/1918	24/03/1918
War Diary	Pozieres-Aveluy	25/03/1918	25/03/1918
War Diary	Martinsart	26/03/1918	26/03/1918
War Diary	Marieux-Domart	27/03/1918	28/03/1918
Heading	19th Divisional Artillery. 87th Brigade R.F.A. April 1918.		
War Diary		01/04/1918	27/04/1918
War Diary	Belle Croix	01/05/1918	07/05/1918
War Diary	Le Biberou	08/05/1918	18/05/1918
War Diary	Dampierre-Sur Moivre	19/05/1918	27/05/1918
War Diary	Bisseuil	28/05/1918	28/05/1918
War Diary	Sarcy	29/05/1918	29/05/1918
War Diary	Chaumuzy	30/05/1918	18/06/1918

War Diary	Hautevillers Vertus	19/06/1918	21/06/1918
War Diary	Thiembronne	01/07/1918	12/07/1918
War Diary	Erny-St-Julien	13/07/1918	31/07/1918
War Diary	Erny-St-Julien	01/08/1918	05/08/1918
War Diary	Lapugnoy	06/08/1918	06/08/1918
War Diary	Bethune	07/08/1918	26/08/1918
War Diary	Nr Bethune	28/08/1918	31/08/1918
War Diary	Locon	01/09/1918	04/09/1918
War Diary	Loisne	06/09/1918	02/10/1918
War Diary	Ligny Le Grand	03/10/1918	03/10/1918
War Diary	Herlies	05/10/1918	15/10/1918
War Diary	Bethune	16/10/1918	17/10/1918
War Diary	Cambrai	18/10/1918	18/10/1918
War Diary	Avesnes Les Aubert	19/10/1918	19/10/1918
War Diary	Haussy	21/10/1918	24/10/1918
War Diary	St Martin	25/10/1918	31/10/1918

WO95/2067

19 Div - 87 Bde
RFA
Jul 1915 - Oct 1918

19TH DIVISION

87TH BRIGADE R.F.A.

JLY 1915-OCT 1918

121/6787

19th Division

87th Brigade R.F.A.
Vol I

July & Aug 15.

Oct '18

Army Form C. 2118

WAR DIARY of 87th F.A. Brigade.

INTELLIGENCE SUMMARY.

(Erase heading not required.)

Instructions regarding War Diaries and Intelligence Summaries are contained in F.S. Regs., Part II. and the Staff Manual respectively. Title pages will be prepared in manuscript.

Place	Date	Hour	Summary of Events and Information	Remarks and references to Appendices
BULFORD	17-7-15	19 a.m.	Entrained at AMESBURY between 2 a.m. and 12 noon. entrained at SOUTHAMPTON.	
	18-7-15		between 6 a.m. and 4 p.m. disembarked at HAVRE where H.Q. & "A" "D" Batteries went into Rest Camp No 5. "C" Battery & B.A.C. into No. 3.	Reference Map.
HAVRE	19-7-15	7 a.m.	Entrained at HAVRE.	HAZEBROUCK 1:50,000
RUMINGHEM	20-7-15	9 a.m.	Arrived at ANDRUICQ, Detrained & went into billets at RUMINGHEM. Weather good. Men billeted in barns. Horses bivouaqued in fields.	
	21-7-15	O.H.D.	Very fine weather.	
	22-7-15	O.H.D.	Same as yesterday. Nothing unusual to report.	
	23-7-15	8 a.m.	Left by road. Starting point road junction by M of RUMINGHEM. On by F of FORÊT D' EPERLECQUES through EST MONT - EPERLECQUES & NG ARDRES - ST. OMER road joining the 57th Infantry Bde. at the road junction just W. of MOULLE (this side of march behind the North Warwicks.) On through TILQUES, ST. MARTIN, ST. OMER, ARQUES to RENESCURE where we went into billets. Weather fine, a few showers.	
RENESCURE	24-7-15	7 a.m.	Left to march by road to HAM-EN-ARTOIS via BLARINGHEM, joined 57th Infantry Bde. at starting point road junction in RENESCURE - BLARINGHEM road E of LYNDE. On through BOESEGHEM, AIRE, MOLINGHEM to HAM-EN-ARTOIS where we billeted.	
		O.H.D.		

Army Form C. 2118

WAR DIARY
or
INTELLIGENCE SUMMARY.
(Erase heading not required.)

Instructions regarding War Diaries and Intelligence Summaries are contained in F.S. Regs., Part II. and the Staff Manual respectively. Title pages will be prepared in manuscript.

Place	Date	Hour	Summary of Events and Information	Remarks and references to Appendices
HAMEN HAUS. OPP.	24-7-15	6 p.m.	Arrived 6 p.m. Weather fine. Horses in fields & Orchards, men in barns. H. QRAS road junction just W. of Church in old convent.	* Reference Map: FRANCE (Paris) sheet 36a. 1/80,000
"	25-7-15	6 p.m.	Weather good, nothing unusual to report.	
"	26-7-15	"	Same as yesterday.	
"	27-7-15	4 p.m.	Inspected in billets by General Sir Douglas HAIG. K.C.B. K.C.I.E. K.C.V.O.	
"	28-7-15	6 p.m.	Weather very warm.	
"	29-7-15	6 p.m.	Weather good. Nothing unusual to report.	
"	30-7-15	6 p.m.	Same as yesterday. Weather showery.	
"	31-7-15	10 a.m.	Same as yesterday. Weather very warm. Left HAM-EN-ARTOIS left road for MERVILLE. Starting point by railway crossing by H.Q. HALTE at 10.10 a.m. on by BUSNES, ST. VENANT joining in with 57th Inf Bde at 2 p.m. at the road junction in the MERVILLE-HAVERSKERQUE road just N.E. of G of HAVERSKERQUE on to MERVILLE where the Infantry left our route, into billets at CHUE DIVELLE at 5 p.m. Bde H.Q. at L.26.a.78. "A"/87 bivouac at L.26.d.16. B/87 L.26.d.26. C/87.L.25.d.12. D/87-L.27.c.55. BAC. L.26.a.71. Water Ford.	
OHA.	1-8-15	5 a.m.	Weather good. Nothing unusual to report.	

2353 Wt. W2544/1434 700,000 5/15 D.D.&L. ADSS/Forms/C.2118.

Army Form C. 2118

WAR DIARY
or
INTELLIGENCE SUMMARY.
(Erase heading not required.)

Instructions regarding War Diaries and Intelligence Summaries are contained in F.S. Regs., Part II, and the Staff Manual respectively. Title pages will be prepared in manuscript.

Place	Date	Hour	Summary of Events and Information	Remarks and references to Appendices
CAMP OUVERTE	1/5/15	6.p.m.	Weather very fine. Nothing unusual to report.	
	2/5/15	6.p.m.	Inspected by Lieut-General Sir James Willcocks, G.C.M.G. K.C.B. K.C.S.I. D.S.O. Batteries drawn up in line at full interval – A.F.D. in field in L.26.c.1.c. C&E in L.6.d.3.1. D.A.C. in their own bivouacs in L.26.d.77. at 3.p.m.	
	3/5/15	"	Weather good	
O.A.D.	4/5/15	"	Weather good, nothing unusual. Captain DRYSDALE & Lt. A.N. JORDAN attached to XIII Bde MEERUT DIV. for 4 days.	
O.A.D.	5/5/15	"	Weather same as yesterday. Captain WILLIAMSON O.A.D.	
O.A.D.	6/8/15	6.43 p.m.	" same as yesterday. Major CATSMITH, Lt. YOUNG, HUNTER attached MEERUT DIV. for 4 days. IXth Bde. MAJOR CAVENDISH. H.C. Lt. POLLOCK. H.M.D. 2Lt. ADDINSELL. A.7. attached to XIIIth IXth IXth Bdes respectively for 4 days.	
H.O.	7.5.15	6.pm	Lt-Col. J.G. DENNISTOUN attached to XIth Bde LAHORE div. for 4 days.	
H.O.	8/5/15	5.pm	Captain H.F. CAULFIELD, 2.Lt. WILSON-HUGHES attached to XIth Bde LAHORE div. for 4 days.	
H.O.	9.5.15	"	Wet then cloudy. Thunder.	
H.O.	10.5.15	"	Weather fine, nothing unusual to report.	
H.O.	11.5.15	"	Captain RAMROD, Lt. COLEMAN. R.A. 2Lt. WAKEFIELD attached XIst X IIIrd & XIst Bdes LAHORE DIV. for 4 days.	
			O.A.D.	

Army Form C. 2118.

WAR DIARY
or
INTELLIGENCE SUMMARY.
(Erase heading not required.)

Instructions regarding War Diaries and Intelligence Summaries are contained in F. S. Regs., Part II. and the Staff Manual respectively. Title pages will be prepared in manuscript.

Place	Date	Hour	Summary of Events and Information	Remarks and references to Appendices
LA HUF DUVELLE	12-8-15	6 p.m.	Weather fine, nothing unusual to report.	
do.	13-8-15	"	Same as yesterday.	
do.	14-8-15	"	2nd Lt SWEET-ESCOTT. S.B. & 2nd Lt STEEDMAN. C.D. attached to LAHORE DIV. 11th Bde also 2nd Lt. SHATTOCK 4th & 6th coys.	
do.	15-8-15	"	2nd Lt WILSON. C.C. & Lt METCALFE. G.H.H. attached to 11th Bde. for 4 days.	
do.	16-8-15	"	Lt MORIARTY posted to A/57th FA Bde.	
do.	17-8-15	"	Weather good nothing unusual to report.	
do.	18-8-15	"	Same as yesterday.	
do.	19-8-15	"	Same as yesterday.	
do.	20-8-15	"	TACTICAL exercise with a view to occupying the CROIX BARBÉE defence system. Battery staffs & B.A.C. & staff. Bde H.Q. at RIEZ BAILLEUL. Visited by G.O.C. R.A. at 2.11 a.m.	
do.	21-8-15	"	Weather showery. Nothing unusual to report.	
do.	22-8-15	"	Very warm day. Received orders to relieve 14 Bde R.H.A. on night 24/25 Aug.	
do.	23-8-15	"	" " Nothing unusual.	
do.	24-8-15	"	" " A Battery & one section each of B, C, & D left billets at 5 a.m.	
	O.H.O.			

WAR DIARY or INTELLIGENCE SUMMARY

Army Form C. 2118

Place	Date	Hour	Summary of Events and Information	Remarks and references to Appendices
	24-5-15		HQrs left billets at 3.30.p.m. by LA GORGUE, LESTREM, LOCON, LES GLATIGNIES to LOISNE. HQ. established in x.22.d.52. A/87 took up position in x.22.d.52. 3/87 right section 4c/87AD/87, right section in x.23.a.93, x.22.d.8.8 and D.F.6.a.20. Remaining sections	Reference Map. Continued BETHUNE 1 to 2000 (B series)
LOISNE	25.5.15. 11.pm 26.5.15. 10.am		came in to join next night round 9.p.m. Zone allotted to Bde from S.27.d.3.8 to A.3.d.20. Batteries registered points in zone.	
	27.5.15 28.5.15. 12noon		Batteries registered their zones. Weather very warm. Group formed:- A, B & C batteries & 2 batteries 86th Bde will come under Lt Colonel WILSON.D.S.O. 86th Bde R.F.A. & D battery 87 group under Lt Colonel KIRBY.DSO. F.A. Bde A/87 ordered to prepare new position in F.6.c.52. one section to be in by 30th inst.	Appendix 91. Appendix No.2
	29.5.15. 1.pm		Zones registered. Battery registered points, A battery fired at working party 150 yds in front of our trenches in A.3.c.44. Weather very fine. Batteries registered Zones.	Appendix N°3
	30.5.15. 12.pm			

O.H.O.

Army Form C. 2118

WAR DIARY
INTELLIGENCE SUMMARY.
(Erase heading not required.)

Instructions regarding War Diaries and Intelligence Summaries are contained in F. S. Regs. Part II. and the Staff Manual respectively. Title pages will be prepared in manuscript.

Place	Date	Hour	Summary of Events and Information	Remarks and references to Appendices
LOOSNE	31.5.18	11 a.m. V.H.D.	B/87 registered from A/87 battery's zone as A/87 moved into new position at 9 p.m. B/87 covered A's zone for the night as well as their own.	Appendix E.
		0.H.D.	D/87 registered (see Appendix)	

No 1.

87th F.A. Brigade (~~~~~~~ Battery~~~~) From 13 noon 32.6.15 to 12 noon 28.6.15

I. Report on operations of the day.

Hour	No. of rounds	Target	Remarks
A/87 3.45 p.m.	29 Shrapnel	Zero Line.	Registering Zone.
C/87 12.5 p.m.	9 "	House in RUE D'OUVERT.	on receipt of orders from Battalion
B/87 9.50 p.m.	27 "	Enemy moving along road from RUE d' MARIAS to RUE D'OUVERT	A.B. movement on the road stopped.

II. Report on Enemy's Artillery

Hour	Weapon	Apparent direction	No. of Shells	Locality Shelled	Remarks
8. a.m.	"	Shells came from			Searching fire was used
10.30. a.m.	5.9	S.E. direction	20	F 6 a 2.4	
3.30 p.m.	How.				

No 2.

I. Tactical Progress Report:

From noon 28th to noon 29.8.15

Time	Target	No. of Rounds stated Lyddite H.E.	Targets	Remarks (on line Points 27)
A/87	3.45 p.m.	23	D.15	
B/87	4.0 p.m.	6 3" Shrapnel	A.3 D.11	
C/87		4	A.3 D.25	
	1.40 p.m.	12	A.3 D.08	
	2.0 a.m.	10	A.3 A.96	
	4.0 a.m.		House S.27 D.27	
A/87	10.30 p.m.	70		Own trenches A.1. A.2.O. enemy's front line trenches between A.3. & B.9. and S.27.A.1. on request of infantry in O.P. Registration Incomplete

II. Report on Enemy's Artillery

Time	Weapon	Approximate position	No. of Shells	Locality shelled	Remarks
A/87 B/87	18 pr		4	-S-	S.27 B.9.
5.0 p.m. 6 p.m.	15 cm.	A/76 B.72 Zun.	3		

Signature

No. 3.

87th F.A. Brigade.

I. Tactical Progress Report

From noon 29.8.15 to noon 30.8.15

Unit	Time	No. of Rounds	Target	Remarks
A/87	12.54. m	28 Shrapnel	A.3.C.4. & large German working party in front of Mendon. Information received from 87/19 Batt.
C/87	noon	12	"	Searching for battalions & ranges S.& 7. D.17.
	12.30 p.m	11	"	Fire at German Trenches 87/2. Infantry. in retaliation for bombardments S.27.D.156
	2.0 p.m	16	"	S.& 7.D.0 & (inclusive) Retaliation 87.2 Infth.
	3.0 p.m	8	"	Registration of Left Barrage. A.A.A. + 1
	3.15 p.m	6	"	Registration of ___ CRATER (Right Barrage) (could not be founded owing to other
	3.25 p.m	7	"	Bdes. ranging on same target.
				Retaliation on Mendon S.27.C.82
9/87	12. noon	6	"	Registration of Mine S.27.D.11
	12.30 p.m	6	"	Fire on Enemy Trench A.3.D. 6.4. (Registering)
	1.15 p.m	4	"	" " A.3.D. 0.8 Lobbing shrapnel
	2.30 p.m	4	"	Enemy Trench A.3.D. 0.8 regarding Southern limit of town
	8.15 a.m	4	"	Communication trench A.3.0.9.5. & A.3.4.5. (Objects visible from army O.P.)
				New front trench. Approx. rights flank of A.C.1. (worrying of infantry)

II. Report on Enemy's Artillery

Time	Weapons	Apparent Positions	No. of Shells	Locality Shelled	Remarks

31/5/15 No 4

Tactical Progress Report

I Report on Operations of the day

Unit	Time	No of rounds	Target	Remarks
B/87	11.30 A.M.	24	Registering sq S28a	Registering sq S28a

II Report on Enemy's Artillery

Time	Weapon	Apparent position	No of rounds	Locality shelled	Remarks
About 9 A.M. at intervals	5-9 How.	Shells coming from S.E direction	7	Searching fire 4 to woods S.E. GORRE.	

J.C Rawcliffe 2/Lt.
Comdg B/87.

Army Form C. 2118.

WAR DIARY
or
INTELLIGENCE SUMMARY.
(Erase heading not required.)

Instructions regarding War Diaries and Intelligence Summaries are contained in F. S. Regs., Part II. and the Staff Manual respectively. Title pages will be prepared in manuscript.

Place	Date	Hour	Summary of Events and Information	Remarks and references to Appendices
LOISNE	1-9-15	12 am / 2.20 pm / 4 pm	Weather showery, rather windy. Nothing unusual to report. A/87 registered from new position in F.5.b.52. O.P. in A.7 & 4.0. B/87 registered Targets do D/87 registered Targets do	Reference Map. BETHUNE. Centered (20.079) 9 Appendices 1.2.3.4. Tactical reports 5.6.7. & 8.9.10.11.
	2-9-15		Fine day. A/87 registered Targets. Weather wild – showery. Retaliation by D+	
	3-9-15	0 hr	A fired at working party+ Fine day.	
	4-9-15		Rather cold day, good deal of rain nothing unusual to report. Tactical reports 8-9-10-11. C/87 day & night at new gun pits.	
	5-9-15	9.30 pm / 0 hr	Fine day, but rather cold. Trench & country very wet & muddy. C/87 moved one section to new position in F.5.6.5.e.x.30 & 47 and OH2 went on digging into the remaining section.	
	6-9-15 / 7-9-15 / 8-9-15	pm	C/87 moved remaining section into new position. Weather good. Nothing unusual to report. Same as yesterday. Some rain.	see 13. 14.

Army Form C. 2118.

WAR DIARY
or
INTELLIGENCE SUMMARY.
(Erase heading not required.)

Instructions regarding War Diaries and Intelligence Summaries are contained in F. S. Regs., Part II and the Staff Manual respectively. Title pages will be prepared in manuscript.

Place	Date	Hour	Summary of Events and Information	Remarks and references to Appendices
LOISNE	9-9-15		Same as yesterday. weather good.	Reference Maps BETHUNE & indexed
	10-9-15		Same as yesterday weather very fine, roads hard and dry	15
O.H.Q.	11-9-15		Same as yesterday. very warm day.	16
O.H.Q.	12-9-15		" " " " Ordered not to use so much ammunition.	17
O.H.Q.	13-9-15		Fine day. Nothing unusual to report.	
O.H.Q.	14-9-15		Same as yesterday – see Tactical progress report	18
O.H.Q.	15-9-15		Same as yesterday. Two A.V.C. Sergeants taken on strength one attached to A/87 one to B/87.	19
O.H.Q.	16-9-15		Two A.V.C. Sergeants taken on strength, one attached to C/87 & D/87.	20
O.H.Q.	17-9-15		Five gunners three drivers received to join deficiencies.	21
			Weather good. Nothing unusual.	
O.H.Q.	18-9-15		Weather good, nothing unusual to report.	22
	19-9-15		Same as yesterday weather good.	23
	20-9-15		Same as yesterday. Received orders at 10 a.m. to start Bombarding Trenches at 7 a.m. till 11 a.m. Orders to W re cut from 2 p.m. with Shrapnel	24 & 25

2353 Wt. W2544/1454 700,000 5/15 D. D. & L. A.D.S.S./Forms/C. 2118.

Army Form C. 2118.

WAR DIARY
or
INTELLIGENCE SUMMARY.
(Erase heading not required.)

Instructions regarding War Diaries and Intelligence Summaries are contained in F. S. Regs., Part II. and the Staff Manual respectively. Title pages will be prepared in manuscript.

Place	Date	Hour	Summary of Events and Information	Remarks and references to Appendices
LOISNE	21/9/15		Started bombardment on German parapets at 9.30 a.m. with H.E. shell. Finished shooting at 12 noon.	
D.H.Q.			Started wire cutting with shrapnel at 2 p.m.	
	22/9/15		All Batteries bombarded parapets with H.E. and cut wire with Shrapnel. Fine day. Germans 9" Howitzer shelled Brigade H.Q. 2nd, not much damage done - 3 horses slightly wounded - 6 rounds H.E. used.	
		3.10 p.m	C/87 position shelled by German HOWITZER - one casualty, gunner severely wounded in chest. H.E. shell used.	
D.H.Q.	23/9/15		Batteries again bombard parapets & cut wire in front of enemy trenches.	
		12 p.m	C/87 again shelled by enemy, 17 rounds shrapnel.	
		7.30 p.m	German HOWITZER again shelled (with H.E) reg'n round Brigade H.Q. shells dropping more to the right, about 8 rounds H.E. probably searching for Anti-aircraft section, line right but about 300 yds short.	
		3 p.m	Two more H.E. dropped in same locality. Fine day, very close, Thunderstorm at about 7 p.m.	
D.H.Q.	24/9/15		All Fine Batteries bombard parapets & cut German wire. Fine day.	

Army Form C. 2118.

WAR DIARY
or
INTELLIGENCE SUMMARY.
(Erase heading not required.)

Instructions regarding War Diaries and Intelligence Summaries are contained in F. S. Regs., Part II. and the Staff Manual respectively. Title pages will be prepared in manuscript.

Place	Date	Hour	Summary of Events and Information	Remarks and references to Appendices
LOISNE			Day of assault	Reference Map Trench 36.S.W.37 36 N.W.1.
"	25.9.15	5.50 am	A/87 fired in support and front trenches alongside A3d11–A3d05 and communication trench A3d66–A4c27. 120 rounds shrapnel. D/87, C/87 in front line and communication trenches, B/87 back line and communication trenches, 50 rounds shrapnel 9.38 H.E. attacked our battery.	
		6.10 am	C/87 in commencement of attack by 58th by Bose formed barrage in communication trench S29c82, S27d41, fired 100 rounds shrapnel B/87 9 q/87 fired 40 rounds shrapnel each in RUE D'OUVERT G.13b.	
	26.9.15		Quiet day no shooting by Brigade. Rain all day.	
	27.9.15		Same as yesterday. Weather bad. Ammunition C/87 shot howitzer left right. Further 9 rounds received from R.A.C. Distributed as follows -	
	28.9.15		A battery 2 – C battery 3 – D battery 4 – B.A.C. 3. Weather bad - rain.	
	29.9.15		Very wet day. Nothing unusual to report. Bombardier NESS D/87 shot in leg by mistake by Gunner GIBBS at D/87 O.P. when comparing with B.C.'s another.	
	30.9.15		Fine day. Cold - rain at night. Nothing unusual to report.	

Army Form C. 2118.

WAR DIARY
or
~~INTELLIGENCE SUMMARY.~~
(Erase heading not required.)

Instructions regarding War Diaries and Intelligence Summaries are contained in F. S. Regs., Part II. and the Staff Manual respectively. Title pages will be prepared in manuscript.

Place	Date	Hour	Summary of Events and Information	Remarks and references to Appendices
LOISNE-3448.		c/o 7	moved back into old position at X22d86	Reference Map BETHUNE contoured ½0000.

2. 4/9/15

Tactical Progress Report 2.

I Report on Operations of the day

Unit: B/87

Time	Nº of rounds	Target	Remarks
5 p.m onwards	14	German trenches about A 3	Retaliation – German was shelling Richard Saillie
8.30 A.M.	5	" Sq. A 3 "	" ditto "

II Report on Enemy's Artillery

Time	Weapon	Nº of rounds	Apparent position	Locality shelled	Remarks
					O.C. 17ᵗʰ Heavy Bty Bde informs me that the 5·9 howitzer I have previously reported is suspected to be on a railway truck & fires from sq A 24 a

H Cavendish Major R.A.
Cmdg B/87

Tactical Progress Report   Evening 2/9/15

I. Report on Operations of the day

Unit	Time	Rds forwarded	Target	Remarks
2/9/15		nil		

II. Report on Enemy's Artillery

Time	Weather	Rds fired	Apparent position & locality shelled	Remarks
Enemy fell from Kaiser from 5 to 6 p.m.		6	FESTUBERT	Wounded men evac. 1 O.R.

Tactical Progress Report   2/4/15

1. Report on Operations of the day

Unit	Time	No of rounds	Target	Remarks
187	5 pm about	18	R.Cruelen Sector Trenches struggling to hold road + Rues des MORTS	
	8.30 A.M. 3/4/15	4	Retaliation on German trenches	

II. Report on Enemy's Artillery

Time	Weapon	No of rounds	Apparent position	Locality shelled	Remarks
5.0 A.M to 0 A.M.	5.9 how.	8	Squares 31 including N.24 & N.24a	LE PLANTIN	(seven were A,C,C,3,0) shells fired from guns near Map Ref 69 (one was a RUE DOUVERT road + square K RUE DOUVERT road + gun was

4·15 p.m. Germans were firing at a Dutch aeroplane + from my O.P. I saw flashes of guns leaving a little to the N.W. of presumably a gun to the N. of homes on the road. She had fire extending the road from a western gun had been seen litting up my training O.P. to my training opposite 117 may be seen and rest be tery ammunition column - from the direction and report of shell it was the gun in ky ground with CRATER

J Cavendish
Maj 2/17

J.F.

Tactical Progress Report

I. Report on the events of the day

Unit	Time	N° of rounds	Target	Remarks
10/1/94		Nil		

II. Report on Enemy's Artillery

Time	Weapon	N° of rounds	Apparent position	Locality shelled	Remarks
8·10 a.m.	Field gun & 5·9 How.	about 30 from 5·9		Bridge over canal F 10 a	Very pretty shooting - bridge not hit - but 3 units horses on road were
midday 2 p.m.	Field gun	6	?	my strumentic tree 400+ in tail of battery	First round effective but no one was at home!

H. Cowardish Maj.

11.

Tactical Progress Report 4/9/15

I Report on Operations of the day

Unit	Time	No of rounds	Target	Remarks
D/87	—	—	—	

II Report on Enemy Artillery

Time	Weapon	No of rounds	Apparent position	Locality shelled	Remarks
—	—	—	—		One "4" Howitzer has again been active, apparently towards GORRE

Wilson Lieut RA
for OC D/87.

Instrument Report on Rifle Shots — 6/4/15
I Report on gun shots in of the day

Unit	Gun	No of rounds	Target	Remarks
0187	4.7"	9	Registering 2 pts N Souton 18... LND 1	

II Report on Enemy's Shelling

Time	Weapon	No of rounds	Approx position of trenches shelled	Remarks
9.10 a.m.	1" 5·9	how are me RSS 1 m about 1 to x w 15		our cas none

J Clanwood hope

13/

7/7/15

Tactical Progress Report

I. Report on operations of the day

Unit	Time	No of rounds	Target	Remarks
0/24	5-30 ?	1	German support front line	Retaliation

II. Report on Enemy's Artillery

Time	Weapon	No of rounds	Apparent position	Locality shelled	Remarks

H Clavend Shafr

14

3/9/15

Tactical Progress Report
I Report on Operations of the day

Unit	Time	No of rounds	Target	Remarks
10/8M	1.30 pm	25	Registration of trenches & wire	
	2 pm	1	German trench	Retaliation

II Report on Enemy's Artillery

Weapon	Time	No of rounds	Apparent position	Locality shelled	Remarks

N Cavendish Major

15

Tactical Progress Report   9/9/15

I Report on Operations of the day

Unit	Time	No of rounds	Target	Remarks
B/87	10.30 a.m.	4	German trenches	Retaliation
	5.30 p.m.	4	S A 3 a 1.4	

II Report on Enemy's Artillery

Time	Weapon	No of rounds	Apparent position	Locality shelled	Remarks

Nil observed here

[signature] OC B/87

10/9/15

Tactical Progress Report

I. Report on operations of the day

Unit	Time	No of rounds	Target	Remarks
10/S.M.	5 p.m.	12	Wire German 2nd line	Registration
	5.45 p.m. onwards	17	Trenches A 3 d	German hit twice at Allies aeroplane
	10.45	12	A 3 d 8 2 & A 3 d 1 3	Two German working parties on their wire
	1.15	8	A 3 d 1 4 3	one " " " " "

II. Report on Enemy's Artillery

Time	Weapon	No of rounds	Apparent position	Locality shelled	Remarks
5 p m	77	4 (2)			Featureless.

H Cartwright Major
Comdg B/87.

16

Tactical Progress Report   12/9/15
I. Report on Operations of the day

Unit	Time	No of rounds	Target	Remarks
9/87.	4.45 p.m.	7	German wire at A4c28	For Identification Registration

II. Report on Enemy's Artillery

Time	Weapon	Apparent position	No of rounds	Locality shelled	Remarks

J Cavendish Major.

17.

Tactical Progress Report   13/9/45

I Report on operations of the day

Unit	Time	N° of rounds in Section	Target	Remarks
D/87	11.30 p.m	2 2 4 4 4	Crossroads S28a33 road at S29a5·5 road at S28b34 Crossroads at S28c78 road at S28c37	Infantry reported a German relief was being carried out at a good deal of movement heard on road from RUE DU MARAIS

II Report on Enemy's Artillery

Time	Weapon	Apparent direction	N° of rounds	Locality shelled	Remarks

JClaverdon Major RFA

Tactical Progress Report   15/9/15
I Report on the actions of the day

Unit	Time	No of rounds	Target	Remarks
D/87	7.15	6	? German [supposed?] [communication?] trenches	An urgent report of infantry who were being bombed.
	8.5	3		

II Report on Enemy Artillery

Time	Weapon	Apparent position	No of rounds	Locality shelled	Remarks

Major R.F.A.
O.C. D/87 R.F.A.

19/

Firing Report from OC C/87d Bae to
OC 87d Bae R.F.A. from 9.0 am
15/9/15 to 9.0 am 16/9/15

Unit	Time	Objective	Amm			Remarks
			S	HE	I	
C/87d	3.PM	A 4 c.1.2 A 5 c.1.1 A 10 G.3.1		16		Avg¹ Observation of fire

R B Trollope Major
C/87 Bae
R.F.A.

Tactical Progress Report

B/87

Time	Target	Rounds
7.15 am 16/9/15	Trench Mortar in house 527.216 at request of infantry.	2

No hostile shelling observed

J. Lumsden

Tactical Progress Report

B/87 Time   Rounds

    2.30 am   527 D.1.6   2
                Enemy's trench
                mortar
                hyrequest of
                Infantry

No hostile shelling observed.

Light very bad from dawn
till 9 am today (17/9/15)

               J Ramsde

N 7

Tactical Progress Report   17/9/15

I Report on operations of the day

Unit	Time	N° of rounds	Target	Remarks
D/8M	4.30 p.m.	4	RUE DE MARAIS S27d15—	Tonight on execution to the 8's urge - report attached
	2.45 a.m.	13	Trenches S27d16— S27d14—	At urgent request of Cheshire Reg'. who were being bombed - left repeated till bombing was stopped

II Report on Enemy's Artillery

Time	Weapon	Apparent position	N° of rounds	locality shelled	Remarks

ACCavendish Major
Comdg D/82

Firing Report from OC. C/87° Bae to
OC. 87° Bae R.F.A from 9.0 am 17/9/15
to 9.0 am 18/9/15

Unit	Time	Objective	Amm'n			Remarks
			S	HE	I	
C/87	2.30 pm	A.3.c.10.6		3		Retaliation
	4.30 pm	A.3.c.10.6		9		Retaliation

Q.d. Addwisell for Capt
7/4.
C/87° Bae R.F.A

(Amended)

Sep 17/8 - 15" Tactical Progress Report   Ref Trench Map 36C
                                                       N.W.I

Unit	Time	No. of Rounds	Target	Remarks
A/67 FA Bde	4.30 PM Sept 17/15	5 Shrapnel	A.3.d.1.4.	Registration

Action by Enemy's Artillery

Time	Weapon	Apparent Position	No. of Shells	Locality Shelled
3.30 pm Sept 17/15	5.9 Howitzer H.E.	Regt. Shells fired 3 fuzes found — no indication shown	11 843	A.8.a.3.9 A.8.a.8.6 junction of No 4 & 5 Communication trenches at Le Plantin

A.W. Wyndham
Capt. R.F.A.
Commanding A/57 FA Bde

Tactical Progress Report 18/9/15

I Report on operations of the day

Unit	Time	No of rounds	Target	Remarks
D/87	4 p.m.	4	Heads of mine	by order of O.C. IND & I
	4.45 p.m	4	RUE DE MARAIS	to ignite herbage

II Report on Enemy's Artillery

Time	Weapon	No of rounds	Apparent position	Locality shelled	Remarks
3.30 p.m	Howitzer	8 H.E.	ABYA19 in front of enemy's front line to trenches to the South East	LE PLANTIN at about midnight to the S-Com trenches	

H Cleverdon
Major R.F.A.
Commanding "D" Battery 87th Brigade R.F.A.

22

Tactical Progress

B/87

        S 27 D 27 (previously reported as
18/9/15   S 27 D 16)
  11 am   On Trench Mortar   3 rds
        by request of Infantry

19/9/15 7.0 am   Same Target   2
                At request of Infantry

19/9/15 9.15 am   Same Target   4 rds

I think this house (known as L 12) ought to be thoroughly destroyed by Howitzers — It gives a great deal of annoyance to the Infantry

                J V Cameron
                      Major

No Hostile Shelling observed
There seems to be a good deal of work going on at A 4 C 85 — I think they are making a redoubt there.

Tactical Progress Report — 21/9/15

I. Report on Operations of the day

Unit	Time	N° of rounds	Target	Remarks
D/87	10.30	7	S 30 c 89	
	11.30	1	Rd Jcln N of Beaupuits + Ran Vivianen A 5 b 5 3	
	11.45	1	S 29 b 9 5 Road Jcln	

II. Report on Enemy's Artillery

Time	Weapon	Apparent position	N° of rounds	Locality shelled	Remarks

_____ Major, R.F.A.
Commanding "D" Battery 87th Brigade R.F.A.

25

Tactical Progress Report   19/9/15

I Report on operations of the day

Unit	Time	No of rounds	Target	Remarks
2/87	10 A.M.	1 oz gun followed by 4	Some hv? Trench near Strand 7	Retaliation on working party of enemy's regiment of infantry who were being worried by trench mortars. The first round happened to be an effective time shrapnel on the numbers of his horse and seemed to stampede. Their men ran out & seemed shattered where to go as they ran in a circle & then disappeared in the trench

II Report on Enemy's Artillery

Time	Weapon	Approx position	No of rounds	Locality shelled	Remarks
2.30 p.m.	4.2 How.	?	9	LE PLANTIN	This may be an effort at the observing stations but I'm inclined to think the fire is drawn by infantry carrying went to on latrine in the S? Com. trench.

JCavendish.

23.

Tactical Progress Report 20/9/15
I Report on operations of the day —

Unit	Time	Nº of rounds	Target	Remarks
—	—	—	—	—

X 29

II Report on Enemy's Artillery

Time	Weapon	Approx position	Nº of rounds	Locality shelled	Remarks
11-1230	5·9 How.	A 24 a.	26.	29 d 27 / 30 c 28	

Wilson Lieut RFA
for Major cmdg D 87.

131/7593

19th Kurdun

Sy: K.B.de: R.7a.
Vol 3
Oct 15

Army Form C. 2118.

WAR DIARY
or
INTELLIGENCE SUMMARY.
(Erase heading not required.)

Instructions regarding War Diaries and Intelligence Summaries are contained in F.S. Regs., Part II. and the Staff Manual respectively. Title pages will be prepared in manuscript.

Place	Date	Hour	Summary of Events and Information	Remarks and references to Appendices
LOISNE	1-10-15		Fine day, cold. All quiet in front nothing unusual to report.	Reference
	2-10-15		Rain all day. Received orders to go into reserve at PARADIS on being relieved by XIIIth Bde R.F.A.	MAP – BETHUNE
	3-10-15		On 3rd & 5th inst. one section each battery relieved by sections of XIIIth Bde batteries at 7 p.m. Relieved sections going into billets at PARADIS	combined sheet 40 NW
	4-10-15		One section each battery relieved by sections of XIIIth Bde Bte at 7 p.m. relieved sections going into billets at PARADIS. XIIIth Bde took over command of Indian II Group at 3 p.m. 77th Bde moving into reserve at PARADIS. Bde H.Q. at Q.17.C.9.3. A battery at Q.30 a 50. B battery at Q.24 a 47. C battery at Q.18.C.45. D battery at Q.18 a 70. B.A.C. moved into billets at Q.18 a 37.	
	5-10-15			
	6-10-15		Fine day. Received orders to move to billets in LES RUES DES VACHES Q.20.Q.21.Q.14.Q.15. On 7th inst. to make room for 58th Inf. Bde	
	7-10-15		Fine day. Brigade moved into billets in LES RUES des VACHES area. H.Qrs at Q.14 a 61 D. A/87 at Q.14 a 63. B/87 at Q.14 b 55. C/87 at Q.20 b 25.	
OHQ				

Army Form C. 2118.

WAR DIARY
or
INTELLIGENCE SUMMARY.
(Erase heading not required.)

Instructions regarding War Diaries and Intelligence Summaries are contained in F. S. Regs., Part II. and the Staff Manual respectively. Title pages will be prepared in manuscript.

Place	Date	Hour	Summary of Events and Information	Remarks and references to Appendices
Rue des VACHES.	7-10-15		D/87 at @ 20 b 4.1. Fine day.	Reference Map BETHUNE Sondouil.
	8-10-15		D/87 changed their billet to @ 19 a 7.7. Fine day.	
	9-10-15		Fine day. Nothing unusual to report.	
	10-10-15		Arrangements made with MD BAC to take 24 of their gunners for instruction for instruction in gun drill by each battery daily.	
	11-10-15		Started work on recovered position at R33 d.7.0. 15 men from each battery & B.A.C. under Lt. WITTENG. 2nd Lt HUNTER R/BAC. Fine day. Working party at recovered position under Lt MORIARTY A/87. 2nd Lt HUNTER D/87.	
	12-10-15		Fine day - very warm. S.L.D. & 2 riding horses received from D.A.C. 1 riding H.D. sent to Artillery. 1 riding to B. 2 LD. to Brattery & 2 to B.HC.	
	13-10-15		Four men posted to Bety from D.A.C. The 2 gunners No 87695 PLUMBLEY. G. and No 15995 DENNINGTON E. sent to C/87. & the 2 drivers No 729. HART and No 64405. WILSON E. to B.A.C. Two gunners from B.A.C. posted to C/87. No 12733 gunner SOUTHWORTH & 92020 gunner HASLAM.	
	14-10-15		Fine day, nothing unusual to report.	
	15-10-15		B/87 attached to MEERUT Divisional Artry. Bright. Gun section moved into	

Army Form C. 2118.

WAR DIARY
or
INTELLIGENCE SUMMARY.
(Erase heading not required.)

Instructions regarding War Diaries and Intelligence Summaries are contained in F. S. Regs., Part II. and the Staff Manual respectively. Title pages will be prepared in manuscript.

Place	Date	Hour	Summary of Events and Information	Remarks and references to Appendices
Q14263D	15-10-15		action at X24a63 on night 15/16 October 1915.	Preference (BETHUNE) combined sheet FRANCE
		Morn	Brigade inspected by G.O.C. R.A. 19th Division. Teams of gunners & column of battery going West at Q3d31. Lieut B Bratton attached to MEERUT Div. Arty.	
	16-10-15		B.S.M. HOLMES. A/87 went in 8 days leave. Left sakin B/87 moved to X24a63.	
	17-10-15		a/BA. N° 33018 LINDSELL B/87 sent on 8 days leave. Fine day.	
	18-10-15	7 a.m.	Lt-Colonel J.G. DENNISTOUN went on 8 days leave. Major H.C. CAVENDISH being left in command of Bde in his absence.	
		4 p.m.	Orders received to move into action in a few days.	
	19-10-15		Two gunners exchanged by B/87. N° 130004 9th DUNNE E & N° 53302 gnr SCOTT. H. for two gunners from 19th D.A.C. N° 72242 9th SIMSON & N° 66793 9th BROWN. Orders received for Bde to relieve 13th Bde.	
			MEERUT DIV. on night 21/2 inst.	
	20-10-15		Fine day, nothing unusual to report.	
	21-10-15		Two sections each "A", "B", & "C"/77 relieved two sections of 2nd 5th & 4th Batteries 13th Bde R.F.A. one section D/87 relieved on return	

WAR DIARY
INTELLIGENCE SUMMARY

Army Form C. 2118.

Place	Date	Hour	Summary of Events and Information	Remarks and references to Appendices
LOISNE	21.10.15		Was relieved 4th Battery. All wagon lines/batteries moved to — A/87 to X15c57. B/87 to X15c20. C/87 to X20c34. D/87 to X15c63. Remaining section D/87 relieved remaining section 14th Battery R.F.A. Remaining sections all 13th B.A.C batteries went out.	Preferred BETHUNE. Continued. MY FRANCE. to see
	22.10.15		Hd.Qrs 37th F.A.B moved to X22d33. O.C. 37th F.A.B took over command of INDIAN I Arty Group which included A/87 F.H.B. at 10 a.m. 87th BAC moved to X16c50. Position of 87 Hos. battery at F5c39. wagon line at X19694. Battery positions at A/77 at F5-5-2. O.P. at A7a40. D/77 at F6a70. O.P. at Q8a17. B/77 at X23 central. O.P. at S20c81. C/87 one section at S14c88, one section moved position at X22d85. O.P at S20c81. Zone covered by INDIAN I artygroup A3d11½ 6S27671½. A/87 covers A3d11½ to A3d09. D/87 covers A3d09 — A3a76. 1 sect C/87.A3a76 to S27c87½. 1 section C/87 enfilades German trenches S27c76 to A3d11½. B/87 covers S27c82½—S27671	
	23.3.15			

Army Form C. 2118.

WAR DIARY
or
INTELLIGENCE SUMMARY.
(Erase heading not required.)

Instructions regarding War Diaries and Intelligence Summaries are contained in F. S. Regs., Part II. and the Staff Manual respectively. Title pages will be prepared in manuscript.

Place	Date	Hour	Summary of Events and Information	Remarks and references to Appendices
LOISNE	21-10-15		Captain CAULFIELD went on leave.	Reference French Map 1/40000
	23.10.15		INDI front line held by two battalions. 10 R. Warwicks on right from A3c12.6 A3a2.6. 7th N. Staffords on left A3a26 to S27c710. A & D/87 support right. B & C/87 support left battalion. Night wire distribution over above zones. One F.O.O. from one of two batteries does F.O.O. for both batteries covering battalion. A/87 Howitzer battery covers whole zone. Batteries registered zones. 1 N.C.O. went on leave from A/87.	
	24.10.15		The following barrages arranged in case of violent attacks. INDI to help INDII arty Group. B/87 to fire on S27d1545-S28a0045. C/87 to fire on S27d3515-S27d1.7 D/87. S27d24-S27c8015. 4.5" How A/87. on gun on A3b6-65 one gun on S27c33. INDII to help 7th Div Arty. A/87 on Hurvoux A3d39, A3d 89, A4c05. A & C/87 on A3d12-A4c03 trench. B & D trench from A4c27-A4c99. Menage asking to triangulate the turn of Rupruit INDI &c	

Army Form C. 2118

WAR DIARY
or
INTELLIGENCE SUMMARY.

(Erase heading not required.)

Place	Date	Hour	Summary of Events and Information	Remarks and references to Appendices
LOISNE	24.10.15		Lt JORDAN B/87 went on weeks' leave. Fine day.	
	25.10.15		Captain H.N.H. WILLIAMSON C/87 went on weeks leave. Lt TROLLOPE left in command of C battery. Fine day. Batteries registered.	
	26.10.15		Lt G. WITTEN H.Qrs. 87th F.A.Bde returned from leave. Fine day, cold. Nothing unusual to report.	
	27.10.15		1. A.V.C. Sergeant N.E. Bde H.Qrs attached to C/87 went on weeks leave. Lt Colonel DENNISTOUN returned from leave & resumed command of INDI Arty Group. Wet day cold nothing unusual to report.	
	28/10/15		Capt B. ORMROD left the brigade to assume command of a section of 19 D.A.C.	
	29/10/15		Lieut H McR. PRECOCK took over as Adjutant of the Bde in place of Capt O.H. ORMROD.	
	30th		This day nothing unusual except a certain amount of enemy arty activity	
	31/10/15		Wet & cold misty. Section of 10/87 Bde relieves a/87 from 1 to 4 a.m. on the front B/87 and section to C/87 Position.	

87th Bde: R.F.A.
P64H

18/7795

On age

19th Kinnear

Nov 15

Army Form C. 2118.

WAR DIARY
or
INTELLIGENCE SUMMARY.

(Erase heading not required.)

87TH T.A. Bde. 1.11.15 — 30.11.15

Place	Date	Hour	Summary of Events and Information	Remarks and references to Appendices
LOISNE	1/11/15		Very wet day. A/87 completed their change of position to C/87 this morning a section of C/87 + whole of B/87 being in same positions.	
	2/11/15		Very wet day. Captn Wilkinson & Lt Jordan returned from leave.	
	3/11/15		Drizzly day. Major Amedroz went on leave. Report from Capt Macleod that the Germans announced by placard that the English might be welcome to their trenches on the 21st. They were reported to have been disparaging language 's whereabout the Kaiser.	
	4.11.15		Intermittent heavy rain.	
	5.11.15		Intermittent sunshine. Lieut Pollock went on leave on the night of the Division & there were themselves up at GIVENCHY. Infantry went on listened this evening ane at at least one point the two men and an officer said something in German then deputed that he would come over.	

WAR DIARY or INTELLIGENCE SUMMARY

Army Form C. 2118

Place	Date	Hour	Summary of Events and Information	Remarks and references to Appendices

6.11.16 — Then was the reply from our side but no venture.
Heavy mist during morning — desultory in afternoon. Majority of officers in our front line trench are of opinion that enemy has evacuated their front line trench in sector at top centre. Craters and killed at GIVENCHY thought to be more strongly manned than usual. Huns continuing to talk of November. Enemy very quiet. Lieut. Khattar went on leave.

7.11.15 — Clear and cold — men shining most of day — shrapnel hampered of RUE DU MARAIS at request of Motor Machine Gun Coast. Enemy quiet. Lieut. Wilson Hughes went on leave. Occasional shrapnel A/89 shelled trench and barricade on RUE DU MARAIS — enemy own carrying wounded away from trench. Enemy quiet.

8.11.15 — Cloud and rain most of day — Enemy artillery active — O.P.7. B+C shelled — no damage —

9.11.15 —

Army Form C. 2118.

WAR DIARY
or
INTELLIGENCE SUMMARY.
(Erase heading not required.)

Instructions regarding War Diaries and Intelligence Summaries are contained in F. S. Regs., Part II. and the Staff Manual respectively. Title pages will be prepared in manuscript.

Place	Date	Hour	Summary of Events and Information	Remarks and references to Appendices
	10-11-15		Rain during early morning - afternoon clear - A/89 located enemy battery. Position shelled and enemy guns silenced. Enemy artillery active - D/87 shelled enemy working party at A.H.b.2.4. Nothing further.	
	11-11-15		Rain most of day - O.P. of A/87 shelled by enemy with 5.9 How, no damage. Retaliation by our Artillery - Very little enemy activity - Sunshine most of day - Enemy artillery very active - also stopped - Retaliation by our artillery was having - especially late in afternoon.	
	12-11-15		Enemy artillery active - Very quiet -	
	13-11-15		Rain and mist all day -	
	15-11-15		Germans attempted to patrol their craters near the their intervening space where the trenches are very close at the Crater. They seemed anxious to show themselves up in small bodies when opportunity offered. Brigade went into rest at St Venant Tramway	

WAR DIARY
or
INTELLIGENCE SUMMARY.
(Erase heading not required.)

Army Form C. 2118

Place	Date	Hour	Summary of Events and Information	Remarks and references to Appendices
	22-27th Nov.		seemed grateful for the change from comparative content of rest billets, were relieved for the time, and more regular habits. Rigging fires & steep came as a very pleasant thing. Inter-Company war began in the wet fields. Hay was drawn from ISBERGUES and firewood from the FORÊT DE NIEPPE. These standings were thoroughly begun and work was proceeding apace when we were called into action	
	24.11.15.		A scheme of training was arranged in which the Brigade was to take part. This was also interfered with owing to our being hurriedly called into action to relieve the 16th Division,	

87th Bde: RFA.
Vol. 5

12/7931

19/4/21

Dec 1915

87th I.A Brigade   Army Form C. 2118.

WAR DIARY
or
INTELLIGENCE SUMMARY.

(Erase heading not required.)

Dec 1 — Dec 31, 1915

Place	Date	Hour	Summary of Events and Information	Remarks and references to Appendices
St Venant	1915 Dec 1 to Dec 3.		Progress at work in horse standings proceeds apace. The men seem free of heat in this work and manifest great enthusiasm in the work. Capt. Williamson started mule standing trestles fashion designed for the section of head cover.	
	Dec 3.	11.20 pm	Received orders at 11.20 pm that 87th Brigade moves up into the line on the front of NEUVE CHAPELLE. First 2 sections to be in action on the night of 3rd/4th December.	
	Dec 4.		Colonel Dennistoun together with Lt Col Thomas, 89th Bde, Major Jones 88th Bde, and Major Strachques 86th Bde left St Venant to reconnoitre the line. The short time left at the disposal of Brigade Commanders necessitates the movements of batteries being made in anticipation. The Battery commanders met Col Dennistoun in the forward area, according to prearranged programme.	
Bocut At Nieppe	Dec 5		Lt Colonel Dennistoun established his Head Quarters.	

Army Form C. 2118.

WAR DIARY
or
INTELLIGENCE SUMMARY.
(Erase heading not required.)

Place	Date	Hour	Summary of Events and Information	Remarks and references to Appendices
Bout de Ville	Dec. 5.		The Left Group consisted of the following batteries. A/87, B/87, C/87, D/87, D/RHA [handed over by the 46th Division of which the 87th Brigade relieved the 3rd London Brigade] together with 3 guns of D/86 acting as heavy gun for A/87, B/87, C/87, and one gun of C/86 acting as heavy gun to D/87, and 6/89 together with 1 section A/89 with heavy gun of A/89 attached to C/89 as the Howitzer artillery of the LEFT GROUP.	
	Dec. 6		Programme of offensive immediately arranged to harass the German. Considered artillery action was carried out between the 4.5" Howitzer batteries and the Field Batteries the former acting against hostile the latter against hostile = Incorrect their might or contain Billets possibly occupied by German at HALPEGARBE and LIGNY.	
	Dec. 7		LE PETIT received great attention. Information received from prisoners who gave themselves over on the night of Dec 6/7 gave the lines of German relief	

Army Form C. 2118.

WAR DIARY
or
INTELLIGENCE SUMMARY.
(Erase heading not required.)

Place	Date	Hour	Summary of Events and Information	Remarks and references to Appendices
Bout de Ville	Oct 7		to be carried out between 8 PM and 9 PM on the night of Oct 7. Prominent artillery of approach were detailed at intervals between these hours.	
	Oct 8		Information from prisoners gave the [?] that our fire produced great casualties among the relieving troops. The German artillery began to be much more active than previously. Apparently this heralded the arrival of more guns on the front. Even of a large caliber guns they seemed to lavish ammunition. Their attention was confined NEUVE CHAPELLE AND PORT ARTHUR. Immediate following enemy was made to bombard our positions.	
	Oct 9			
	Dec 10		Notes failed bombardment was continued at odd intervals. Construction of Comic An line of LEFT GROUP was commenced. This successful operation was carried on under the supervision of Lieut E B Sweet-Escott	

WAR DIARY or INTELLIGENCE SUMMARY.

(Erase heading not required.)

Place	Date	Hour	Summary of Events and Information	Remarks and references to Appendices
Bout- de Ville	Dec 11		Weather continued to be uncertain after a spell of moderately clear weather. Observation improved from this date, with a minimum barometer of 29.3	
	Dec 12		Actions excepted for during a partial attack in German front line in front of THE N E 8. had approx BOAR'S HEAD. The 59th Infantry Brigade were to have carried our the partial invasion of the enemy trenches. This attack was postponed beyond the end of the month. German field work known as cupola near its approaches near FERME DU BIEZ. A large earthwork encircles by a parade & platform connected with a raised approaches (witnesses line of the many pill boxes the Hun intend to keep strongly manning the intermediate positions)	
			glass hire.	
	Dec 13th		Recent efforts appear in the Turners front. This are of a much less offensive nature than the	

Army Form C. 2118.

WAR DIARY
or
INTELLIGENCE SUMMARY.
(Erase heading not required.)

Instructions regarding War Diaries and Intelligence Summaries are contained in F. S. Regs., Part II. and the Staff Manual respectively. Title pages will be prepared in manuscript.

Place	Date	Hour	Summary of Events and Information	Remarks and references to Appendices
Bout d Ville	Dec 26		Prussian Guard when they succeeded.	
	Dec 23		52nd Infantry Brigade relieved us in trenches before NEUVE CHAPELLE. Enemy's systematic bombardment of houses, O.Ps. is intermittent.	
	Dec 25		Unusual parties on the part of French was apparent. Germans moved keep over their parapet began to shout whereon aim were strictly compliance with by the artillery on this front.	
	Dec 27 -30.		Harassing operations were systematically carried out on this front. Estimates billets at HAUT POMMEREAU, LIGNY, LE PETIT, HALPEGARBE were effectively dealt with. The New year heralded by several batteries by 19 rounds at 5 minutes to 12 and 16 rounds 5 minutes after.	
	Dec 31			

Sykes Coll: R.F.A.
Vol: 6

Army Form C. 2118.

WAR DIARY
or
INTELLIGENCE SUMMARY.
(Erase heading not required.)

Place	Date	Hour	Summary of Events and Information	Remarks and references to Appendices
Bertrancourt	1916 Jan. 1		Fairly quiet on both sides. Nothing special to report.	
"	2		Light was very bad all day. B/87 very busy registering their zone from the new battery position - M 26 a 5.0. Bombing attack did not take place - wind was away 2nd Lts. Eldridge & Bell proceeded to the Base. Fairly quiet on both sides -	
"	3		The bombing attack did not take place owing to the continuous shortage of the night. The batteries were obliged to retaliate a good deal in consequence of the Huns shelling our trenches - A/86 joined the Left Group. Relieving the two positions at the old post occupied by the 9th London as L.R.H.A. came out of action on the 3rd.	
"	4		B/86 went to the Group did excellent work registrating on the zone covered by B/87. All other batteries quiet. Hostile aeroplanes over - A very dull day. General Fitz Maurice called on Colonel Dennistoun. The fourth gun returning to A/86 arrived -	
"	5		Dull, cold & wet day - General Twyford called on Colonel Dennistoun. General Fitzmaurice visited O.P. 241 rounds fired by guns of Left Group chiefly with the scheme of aggression	
"	6			
"	7			

Army Form C. 2118.

WAR DIARY
or
INTELLIGENCE SUMMARY.
(Erase heading not required.)

Instructions regarding War Diaries and Intelligence Summaries are contained in F.S. Regs., Part II. and the Staff Manual respectively. Title pages will be prepared in manuscript.

Place	Date	Hour	Summary of Events and Information	Remarks and references to Appendices
Bout de Ville	1916 Jan. 8		A/86 registering their zone – Whilst doing so they had a premature which wounded a Sergt of the 11 Munster. The football came the bursting of the shell case over to its being too close for the bore. Weather conditions were good. The enemy did a good deal of firing especially with 5.9 How round about Nerve Chapelle. Nil also of Richbourg. There was noticeable that they fired as usual and in did so evidently the times we ran short of ammunition. On the whole quiet on the C.B.'s in	
	9		Nerve Chapelle We are promptly retaliation the enemy fired a few gas shells on our front line trenches. House S17 a.8.8 is a very Boche sniper – always promptly retaliation.	
	10		B/87 fired for registration only. Enemy 77mm were very active – also snipers – Light was good for observing.	
	11		At 7 a.m. the Smoke Demonstration Scheme took place, all batteries of the left Group taking part with the Infantry at a given time and made Barrage were formed whilst the idea of inducing the enemy to man his front line trenches, to be fired on by our batteries. This was	

2353 Wt. W2544/1454 700,000 5/15 D.D. & L. A.D.S.S./Forms/C. 2118.

WAR DIARY
or
INTELLIGENCE SUMMARY.
(Erase heading not required.)

Army Form C. 2118.

Place	Date	Hour	Summary of Events and Information	Remarks and references to Appendices
Bout de Ville	Jan 11th (contd)		however is too well known & the enemy side apparently did not man their parapets as was expected. There was also a feint at the Boars Head in the afternoon at 3 p.m. which did not evoke much [response?]	
	12		Very quiet indeed on both fronts. A little retaliation on both sides to report. The late attempts to "carry" the Hun line at Loos has useful in explaining the fact that the Huns on this front are as wary & attentive as us on this part of them & as powerful as of the O.C. C/07 their armaments of Barrage is excellent to a degree—their supply of ammunition is equal to ours and the same apparently as ours	
	13	4.20 a.m Jan 18 hrs	Conditions bad for observation and shooting own to wind and rain. There is a new gap at S11.d 4.5. A good many German run has lately seen on the Lorgies Road	
	14		Light was bad today. Our Artillery did a good deal of firing today in the way of aggression and hoping today spots open - the enemy were quiet and did not seem inclined to retaliate.	

WAR DIARY
or
INTELLIGENCE SUMMARY.
(Erase heading not required.)

Army Form C. 2118.

Place	Date	Hour	Summary of Events and Information	Remarks and references to Appendices
Bout de Ville	14 (con'td)		One enemy plane flew over our lines from the direction of Erclaines. It attacked ~~Wingles~~ of 121st Brigade 38th Div, and reported as getting ¾ths hang of their statues. All non quiet & very little firing done on either side —	
"	15.		A/89 & D/107 fired in conjunction at German support trenches & suspected battery position at T7c1.8½ — added product a good deal of retaliation. Flashes of a German Machine gun were located at S5b7/7.5½. A/89 gun battery firing from S30d0.2. but out of its direction range. A poor day for observing, though there was a good deal of firing on both sides —	
"	16		100 rounds were expended by the unit cutting section of D121 & a lane was cut at S10b.9.1 — It is being very good, there were a good many planes of both hostile & friendly, added our own took to our own — In the afternoon very little firing was done as the ?? was going so fast. Col. Dennistoun left & came & Col. Thomas of the 89th Brigade took over command of the staff Group. D/107 fired 231 rounds at front lines & went at S5b.6.3. N. bd was exceptionally quiet & a good	
"	17			
"	18			

Army Form C. 2118.

WAR DIARY
or
INTELLIGENCE SUMMARY.
(Erase heading not required.)

Instructions regarding War Diaries and Intelligence Summaries are contained in F.S. Regs., Part II. and the Staff Manual respectively. Title pages will be prepared in manuscript.

Place	Date	Hour	Summary of Events and Information	Remarks and references to Appendices
Bois de Ville	18	contd	...of material damage was done. Df 887 position & bullets were shelled but no men wounded. Otherwise as always.	
	19		Our Artillery more active than usual. Today some of our Batteries carried out Col Thomas scheme to arrange to reach (so nearer) the Bois du Biez, with the idea (I think) a hidden battery & O.C. The effort was good as there fire caused as soon as the wood was fired on. Light was very good throughout the day and no consequence there were several places etc. One escaped an aim & proceeded in the direction of Lorn. A good deal of firing on both sides.	
"	20		In accordance with Div Schon all billows fired three salvos at 2 a.m & 3.10 a.m on their nght lines. Several hostile aircraft were observed in the morning. The Mushroat Mound (S67J3) undoubtedly a very shay place & so far the Howitzers &c. &c. not made much effect on it. Light was good.	

2353 Wt. W2544/1454 700,000 5/15 D.D. & L. A.D.S.S./Forms/C. 2118.

Army Form C. 2118.

WAR DIARY
or
INTELLIGENCE SUMMARY.
(Erase heading not required.)

Instructions regarding War Diaries and Intelligence Summaries are contained in F.S. Regs., Part II. and the Staff Manual respectively. Title pages will be prepared in manuscript.

Place	Date	Hour	Summary of Events and Information	Remarks and references to Appendices
Boisdinghem	21		Colonel Thomas off to Corps. Col. Wilson Catlin in Command 17th Bn. return of Col. Dennistoun. Bulletin. Weather depressed to day of billets, wet and cold. to be on the other side of Hannekes — to day of the Bn. of probably taking place on the 30th. Winter of 12.15 — Lt. Extremely good — collar proven in the afternoon. O.C. A/06 to counsel that the forward at S6883 contain O.C. on the firing out normally where the relation — our batteries did a lot of aggressive work, set as firing in suspicious O.C.'s machine gun emplacements etc —	
"	22		Batteries for our regstering fixed. asked their own zones, in accordance with Col. Thomas idea, so that in the case of counter-attack they will be able to he carried out some effort he took down at cross roads M27d7.9 near billets, to make down from the new French guns way to fact that Bn. one billets to this asunny from Cubres Ridge the day was exceptionally quiet on attention. There are probably battery position that the Bois de Ray.	

WAR DIARY or INTELLIGENCE SUMMARY

Army Form C. 2118.

Place	Date	Hour	Summary of Events and Information	Remarks and references to Appendices
Bout de Ville	Jan 23		The light was too bad for accurate observation. The aeroplanes were very active. Enemy Artillery unusually quiet.	
"	24		From the B.1.3 was seen to be on fire during the afternoon. Our own Artillery did some firing in the way of Registration of targets outside our Lines and a certain amount of aggression. There is at least two new O.Ps. in Bois du Biez. Two new covered O.Ps. The work of building O.Ps. is growing apace. There are in the way of construction. Hostile Artillery unusually quiet.	
"	25		Enemy Artillery not quiet. The heavy put in some good work at S.1147 in Distance the flash of a four gun battery was observed near Beau Puits. Two enemy aeroplanes worked on being engaged. Two German balloons up at Wingles & T.21.b. Bullets landed over the representation of Batteries & Ammn Col. - It killed 21. It taken on our line. See S.120 & Brigade R.F.A.	
—	26		From day 7. 8½ suspected O.P. The standard that was being erected against a post tree in Bois du Biez at S.6.a.5.2 has been removed. S.17a.7.8½ suspected O.P.	

Army Form C. 2118.

WAR DIARY
or
INTELLIGENCE SUMMARY.
(Erase heading not required.)

Instructions regarding War Diaries and Intelligence Summaries are contained in F.S. Regs., Part II. and the Staff Manual respectively. Title pages will be prepared in manuscript.

Place	Date	Hour	Summary of Events and Information	Remarks and references to Appendices
Beit to Hill 26	Jan (cont'd) 26		It is rumoured that the enemy are massing at Don. He intends formation of Col. Wilson is prepared for this being the return of the enemy from recent shows by ½ & how far & to what extent on this front. By 10/pr. Shrapnel fire - L.G.F. was quite good.	
" "	27		At 11.15 a.m. enemy's artillery became very active on our trenches. This appeared was no doubt due to the good work our Heavy Howitzers guns had been doing during the last two days. D/87 fired 210 rounds a previous retaliation. A fast which seems to prove that our full gun fire to take effect on a electric the kind of it is a determined means that the enemies mis only can be counter on to shell the enemy or the enemy- the power of the enemy was thoroughly concentrated on the North side of the N.E.B. Hosts of a form Gun Battery was observed at Sted 27 Remarkably clear fine day. Major General Commanding D/87 took over the command of the Brigade via Lt Colonel Whin, who alone is strong of General Fitz Maurice - Commander the Divisional Artillery.	

Place	Date	Hour	Summary of Events and Information	Remarks and references to Appendices
Bethune	28		Dull morning - fires later - the new Steel loop-hole Gas pits in course of construction on many emplts to obviate being too exposed on x-t above seam cult aerial observation as t it's conspicuousness - Q/121 rm firing at parapets & reported nearly 100 with good results. It Heavies on our right front at J10c95, held up a lot of parapet.	
"	29		Dull day - during the previous night a Group saken took place - all batteries took part, & fired on various points with apparent success. Quiet during the day.	
"	30		Our Artillery fired frequently during the day at request of Infantry Cos, for day. The 88 took over the major part of the batteries and all batteries were out.	
Haverskyn	31		Most colder. All batteries took over from ettes on the relief and of Haverskyn and the 30th Dist 117 D relieved the left Coys of the 19th Division	

WAR DIARY
or
INTELLIGENCE SUMMARY.
(Erase heading not required.)

Army Form C. 2118.

Place	Date 1916	Hour	Summary of Events and Information	Remarks and references to Appendices
Mamarise	Feb 1.		The whole Brigade is now in rest at Caori Maraise and round about	S.D.58.
	2		Colonel Denniston returned from leave. All Batteries occupied in a General cleaning up and renewing of all gear	S.D.59
	3.		Programme of training being carried out	S.D.58
	4		O.C. Brigade inspected A/87 & D/87 & 2 Lts gun team in action at open battle	″
	5		Programme of training in full swing	S.D.58
	6		Specially scheme took place. All the Artillery of the division took part. This was to carry out the General idea of communication by wind signal in the case of an attack	S.D.58
	7		When the Infantry & Artillery had to H.Q. O.C. Brigade inspected C/87 and A/87 & gun team in action at open battle	S.D.58
	8		O.C. Brigade inspected Ammo Col en march	

WAR DIARY
or
INTELLIGENCE SUMMARY.

(Erase heading not required.)

Army Form C. 2118.

Place	Date	Hour	Summary of Events and Information	Remarks and references to Appendices
Goris-Mazraa	9		Programme of training being carried out as preparation for inspection of G.O.C. R.A.	A/9
	10		The G.O.C. R.A. inspected all the Batteries & Ammn. Colms. of the Bgde. and appeared entirely satisfied at the condition of the men, horses, vehicles etc. It was mentioned to officers —	A/9
	11		Any cold dull day. Ordrs. recd. yesterday that in all probability Col. [?] will command the Bgde. and Capt. [?] Col Joe's to [?] A.D. instead of Major [?]	A/9
	14		Punctuality invariably into time Lawrence with one section of Dunning out the time to the back of the scheme of Brussels canal the Orpheus teaches of the 10th R.A. Arty. relieving the [?] Arty now given up in favor of assist at the Ryal Salute of the Sard. but. 8/67 and D/67 were sent to	A/9

Army Form C. 2118.

WAR DIARY
or
INTELLIGENCE SUMMARY.
(Erase heading not required.)

Instructions regarding War Diaries and Intelligence Summaries are contained in F. S. Regs., Part II. and the Staff Manual respectively. Title pages will be prepared in manuscript.

Place	Date	Hour	Summary of Events and Information	Remarks and references to Appendices
CROIX MARMEUSE	14		NEW LEFT GROUP 38th Div under Colonel Head A/87 and C/87 placed under the command of RIGHT GROUP. Single section of fair battery mounts into the line.	ay
	15			ay
CROIX MARMEUSE	16		87th Bde HQ established at CROIX MARMEUSE	ay
	20		B/87 and D/87 withdrawn from 38th Div and placed under the command of RIGHT and LEFT GROUP. 10" Am Infantile.	ay
	24		Section of B/87 advanced in support position on RUE DU BOIS. Ammunition for 3 days. Stevens continuous intermittent.	ay
	26		Thaw with steady barometer slightly falling.	ay
	28		D/87 advanced to an advanced position in LAFAYETTE.	ay

WAR DIARY or INTELLIGENCE SUMMARY

Army Form C. 2118.

87 Div R.F.A. XIX Vol 8

Place	Date	Hour	Summary of Events and Information	Remarks and references to Appendices
CROIX MARMEUSE	MARCH 1		Two captive enemy sausage balloons escaped on from PULLUCH travelling N.W. towards the sea.	
	2		Raw atmosphere developing to a drizzle in the afternoon	
	3		Fair clear atmosphere	
	4		Enemy very tranquil. 9 am - 9 am being 18th minor attempts to induce the enemy to show himself were attended with ambiguous success. Ammunition shown on our parapet drew hostile sniper.	
	5			
	6		B/87. (one section) advanced to wire cut to position in front of LORETTO RD. gun position occupied for the night and day only. ARTY	
	7		Colonel Rennie took over command of RIGHT GROUP. 19/D	
	8		R/87 advanced to forward position at ANGERIE.	
	9		Lieut. W.R. Young Flying arm Rifleman leaving ?	
	10			

Army Form C. 2118.

WAR DIARY
or
INTELLIGENCE SUMMARY.
(Erase heading not required.)

Instructions regarding War Diaries and Intelligence Summaries are contained in F.S. Regs., Part II. and the Staff Manual respectively. Title pages will be prepared in manuscript.

Place	Date	Hour	Summary of Events and Information	Remarks and references to Appendices
CROIX.	10		Wounded by H.E. shell near CHAMPIGNY FARM. LIEUT. COLEMAN. was evacuated to No. 2. C.H. thence to No. 12. Stationary Hospital BOULOGNE.	W
MARMUSE.			* for Biographical note, see Annexe. Suitres Summary	
	13		Lt. Col. J.C. Denniston's demi's command of RIGHT 19TH BATTY GROUP 19th Div. thro'up Lt. Col. D.G. Wilson's return from leave to England.	Us
	18.		Leave re-opened.	
Latoulon	25		Col. Denniston took over command of Right Group, fm Col. Mure, 25th Div. Group consists of following batteries. — "I" R.H.A - B/17, D/87, B/120, C/122.	
	26.		Relief completed C/179, 39th Div. provided a waggon day for "I" R.H.A.	

WAR DIARY
or
INTELLIGENCE SUMMARY.

Army Form C. 2118.

Place	Date	Hour	Summary of Events and Information	Remarks and references to Appendices
Lacouture	March 27		Work on O.P.'s started under Lieut Bremridge R.E. 225th Co. 39th Divn. Watering parties provided daily by the Group.	
"	28		Both sides very quiet, a number of fires were observed in rear trenches at S.11.d.4.8.; weather good for observation.	
"	29		Hostile Battery located at T.26.a. 17°.40' Right of Laquis Church. One gun was seen to fire twice during the day, 3 men were seen moving about outside their dug-outs.	
"	30.		Enemy Artillery fairly active. CAVENDISH SQUARE got third hit ab 5.9. but no damage to O.P. Italia. Very little activity to whats on our side.	
"	31		New type of German flares seen right own own lines, quiet a ball, sides.	

※

Lieut R.A. Coleman 2nd Lo R E. enlarged Monmouth
Engineer Liverpool. After travelling in America and in
Canada he finished the 0.7.14 B.J. 79 B.a.
12th Oct 1914.

2353 Wt. W2544/1454 700,000 5/15 D.D. & L. A.D.S.S./Forms/C. 2118.

87 R.F.A

87 F.A. BDE.
WAR DIARY
or
INTELLIGENCE SUMMARY.

Army Form C. 2118.

Vol 9

XIX

Place	Date	Hour	Summary of Events and Information	Remarks and references to Appendices
LACOUTURE	April 1.		Weather fine & warm. Much activity seen at PIANO HOUSE, & supplies and large wagons were in progress. A German [crossed out] Plane over, shot down at 6.50 a.m, & fell 1 mile north of RUE DU BOIS.	An
"	2.		Weather continues fine, but very thingy. Very little to report; both sides quiet. Work on O.P.'s continues, and more 20 mm. work during the night & 25 during the day.	An
"	3.		Nothing unusual to report. 30 men from D.A.C. attached to D/87 to work on alternate positions.	An
"	4.		Hostile artillery quiet during day. Weather much cooler, dull in afternoon -	
"	5.		Weather fine but cold, nothing unusual to report.	

Army Form C. 2118.

WAR DIARY
or
INTELLIGENCE SUMMARY.
(Erase heading not required.)

Instructions regarding War Diaries and Intelligence Summaries are contained in F.S. Regs., Part II. and the Staff Manual respectively. Title pages will be prepared in manuscript.

Place	Date	Hour	Summary of Events and Information	Remarks and references to Appendices
LACOUTURE	6		Enemy shelled Hersten & Rue du Bois with 98 c.m.m. shells, very little damage done. This is the first appearance of 4.2's c.m.m. on this front.	S/Cr
"	7		Weather fine, but misty. Is observation, Enemy shelled Bn-Bn. H.Q. with 5.9's, having two men, otherwise no damage done.	(a)
"	8		Enemy antiaircraft shell fell on 10/97th Wagon Lines killing few horses & wounding three slightly. Our Drive was rather luck hit in the foot. Enemy enfiladed our Front Line in the vicinity of Sap. Trench with 77 m.m., wounding three men. This gun probably fires from Chapelle St. Roch.	(a)
"	9.		Quiet day, nothing unusual to report.	
"	10.		ditto ditto	

2353 Wt. W2544/1454 700,000 5/15 D.D. & L. A.D.S.S./Forms/C. 2118.

Army Form C. 2118.

WAR DIARY
or
INTELLIGENCE SUMMARY.
(Erase heading not required.)

Place	Date	Hour	Summary of Events and Information	Remarks and references to Appendices
LA COUTURE	April 11		Lieut Turgeon 5th Inf Bde. Scout Officer captured three Germans at a listening post, one being an officer - another German was killed.	
"	12		Infantry made a successful trenches raid on enemy trench line opposite Richebourg l'Avoué, about 30 Germans were killed.	
	13		A/87 were shelled about 10.30 am until 4.25; no damage was done to the Battery, but an Infantry officer passing at the time was badly hit by the enemy. It is probable that the enemy were searching for the Indian arty - who have a section on the road about 40 yds south of A/87.	
	14		Quiet day, nothing unusual to report. One section of A/87 & C/87 relieved by Battery of 32nd Div. Art.	

WAR DIARY
or
INTELLIGENCE SUMMARY.
(Erase heading not required.)

Army Form C. 2118.

Place	Date	Hour	Summary of Events and Information	Remarks and references to Appendices
	April			
LACOUTURE	15.	-	A/87 & C/87 proceeded to rest billets at HAVERSKERQUE which were vacated by them on 14th Feb. Stop placed by D/87 batteries	/A/
"	16		B/87 returned by D/87. 30th Div. not prepared to rest but at HAVERSKERQUE	D/4
HAVERSKERQUE	17.	-	Batts. rested after continuous strain which lasted from Sec 3rd till hereinunder almost without a break.	A/4
	19.		Billeting area reconnoitered in place of HAM EN ARTOIS. Finally settled at THEROUANNE and adjoining villages	
	21.		Central billets in THEROUANNE area. A/87 and Amm. Col. 87 billetted in WESTRE HEM B/87 and C/87 in NIELLES, D/87 UPEN D'AVAL	

WAR DIARY
or
INTELLIGENCE SUMMARY.

Place	Date	Hour	Summary of Events and Information	Remarks and references to Appendices
THEROUANNE	23		Easter Sunday. Joint wires 586? and 87 Bde RFA Bde training for the open battle. Continued section & Battery training. Training of Batt Staff & minor officers	
	24 to 28			
	29 to 30		Brigade training under Brig Genl Forster, advance on ENQUINEGATTE (supposed)	
			Divisional training under Major Genl T. Bridges. Secondary testing signallers and communications.	

To
A.Gs.Office
  at the Base

J.D.164.

  Herewith War Diary for may 1916, also complete and up-to-date nominal roll of the whole Brigade.

8/6/16.

[signature]
LIEUT-COLONEL. R.F.A.
COMMANDING 87th.F.A.BDE..

87th. F.A. BRIGADE.
NOMINAL ROLL OF OFFICERS, W.Os. N.C.Os. & MEN.

RANK.	NAME.	REMARKS.
LT-COL.	J.G. Dennistoun R.F.A.	Commdg. 87th. F.A. Bde.
Lieut.	G.L. Wilson. " "	Adjutant " "
Lieut.	E Wilson-Hughes " "	Orderly Officer. " "

ATTACHED.
Captain. H.E. Griffiths. R.A.M.C.

NUMBER.	RANK.		REMARKS.
92579.	R.S.M.	Brown	F.
18149.	Staff S.	Howard	J.
46174.	" "	Mutch	J.
52550.	a/Sgt.	Davis	G.
16818.	Corpl.	Roberts	A.
18216.	Bombr.	Curtis	W.
18676.	a/Bdr.	Barrow	H.
46318	s/a/Br	Whitlock	G.
1596.	"	Heath	W.
13055.	"	Adams	R.H.
1069.	Gunner.	Knight	H.E.
96866.	"	Power	J.
18699.	"	Robinson	E.R.
64662.	"	Saywell	G.
12989.	"	Sissions	H.
86022.	"	Williams	T.
12301.	"	Wilson	E.
12615.	"	Bedson	A.
73249.	"	Ellis	P.
19611.	"	Taylor	D.
13001.	Driver.	Bain	W.
19244.	"	Beeton	J.
5927.	"	Casey	J.J.
92425.	"	Chapman	A.
18693.	"	Clougher	J.
13248.	"	Cornick	E.
12587.	"	Davenport	A.
12435.	"	Hardacre	R.
17440.	"	Leeds	F.
560.	"	McCrorie	J.
71573.	"	Mitchell	L.M.
64342.	"	Pidgeon	A.
13173.	"	Sanger	F.
90746.	"	Sanger	C.
17437.	"	Self	H.
18474.	"	Mason	W.E.
64304.	"	Pullan	H.
12890.	"	Powell	R.
64431.	Gunner.	Johnson	J.
18790.	"	Taylor	W.

ATTACHED.

635.	Staff Sgt.	Herbert	W.T.
91782.	s/a/Bdr.	Nolan	R.
85972.	Gunner.	Saxton	F.
64126.	"	Johnson	R.
8569.	"	Simmonds	E.
28339.	"	Evans	W.
25962.	"	Barker	H.

Interpreter. Liemgaux

7/6/16.

Dennistoun
LT-COLONEL. R.F.A.
COMMANDING 87th. F.A. BRIGADE.

A/87th

Nominal Roll
of Officers W.O.s & N.C.O.s & Men of A/87 F.A. Bde

Reg. No	Rank	Name		
	Major	A.I. Drysdale		
	Lieut	W.G. Hutt		
	2/Lt.	T.A. Charlesworth		
	Do	C.A. Hawke		
	Do	D. Farquharson		
50667	B.S.M.	W.T. Holmes		
13105	Q.M.S.	T. Gailey		
30496	Farr Serj	L.W.C. Carroll		
79945	Serj	J. Lane		
64321	Do	T.J. Wright		
34158	Do	G. Clarke		
35307	Do	F. Sowell		
74379	Do	E.J. Norman		
41963	Corpl	J.W. Crabtree		
50700	Do	F. Butler		
30700	Do	J. Cummins		
5781	Do	W.H. Quilliam	at present in Hospital England	not struck off strength
61265	Saddler Corpl	W. Sheppard		
99037	Shoeing Smith Corpl	A.D. Fowler		
36790	Bomb	J.B. Higginbotham		
13063	Do	M. Jones		
17431	Do	L.J. Dury		
12855	Do	W. Evans		
36902	Do	H.A. Dalby		
12074	Do	G.C. Asher		
54806	Do	D.C.H. Collins		
61927	a/Bdr	A.T. Gill		
18092	D	L. Kate		
19032	D	W. Kite		

Nominal Roll (cont'd)

Reg. No.	Rank	Name
124811	A/Bdr	C. Wood
58118	Do	J. Saunders
64251	Do	E. Wilkinson
64192	Do	M. Parker
106295	Do	E.G. Tavum
37413	Gunner	H. Bailey
13255	Do	E. Birt
75096	Do	A.J. Bowen
31603	Do	E. Bray
46446	Do	A.G. Brodie
32510	Do	A. Brooks
37142	Do	F. Brown
12528	Do	G. Cadwell
13087	Do	E. Carlson
12842	Do	J. Cartwright
86514	Do	A. Chadwick
88986	Do	A. Chamberlain
12586	Do	W. Clough
33320	Do	F. Cross
7073	Do	A. Cosgrieve
36860	Do	L. Cogley
54419	Do	A.R. Collins
25522	Do	T. Doyle
37022	Do	W. Downer
36996	Do	J. Eccles
50806	Do	W. Ede
27606	Do	W.J. Edmonds
64375	Do	H. Somersall
92044	Do	A. Harrison
13609	Do	J.H. Heald
89946	Do	T. Heaney
36807	Do	J.W. Hill

Nominal Roll (cont)

Reg No	Rank	Name
19985	Gr	J. E. Hilton
13051	Do	A. Holland
55761	Do	W. D. Hooton
64387	Do	H. Ingram
36505	Do	A. E. Horne
64126	Do	R. Johnson
50911	Do	R. W. Jones
36391	Do	T. Jones
86453	Do	H. Loe
19397	Do	H. Lawrence
13030	Do	E. McIntyre
12210	Do	J. A. McKie
62605	Surveyor/Plotter	J. Morgan
16763	Gr	F. S. O'Neil
5989	Do	F. A. Palmer
58158	Do	F. Reeves
29491	Do	E. Roberts
52302	Do	F. Scott
86607	Do	J. Shepherd
61168	Do	J. V. Spurring
18395	Do	F. Stopford
54651	Do	A. Sturgess
13282	Do	R. Thomas
69410	Do	J. E. Tolladay
17339	Do	E. Turner
37045	Fitter	G. A. Griffiths
16962	Wheeler	F. Stone
57875	Saddler	H. A. A. Thompson
99160	Shoeingsmith	G. A. Davis
106154	Do	J. Cumming

Nominal Roll. (cont'd)

Reg No	Rank	Name
12878	Driver	A. Goodman
12365	Do	R. Brown
5923	Do	G. Bryan
1747	Do	S. L. Chidgey
5787	Do	C. J. Clarey
5780	Do	J. C. Cruphey
26596	Do	D. R. Craven
36380	Do	J. Crawford
11987	Do	A. A. Day
12884	Do	W. Downes
18417	Do	A. Dugdale
37254	Do	Jos Dyer
64218	Do	J. A. Farley
50212	Do	F. W. Ferrell
64221	Do	A. Greenfield
19251	Do	W. Graham
12965	Do	T. Griffiths
19543	Do	W. H. Hayward
64224	Do	J. W. C. Hall
12966	Do	Ed Houghton
12476	Do	J. C. Hurst
64231	Do	T. W. Jarvis
92010	Do	O. C. Jones
37321	Do	T. Keeley
13018	Do	J. G. Kelly
18394	Do	R. Lee
18451	Do	Wm Leigh
12217	Do	W. Lewis
12343	Do	H. Lomas
37861	Do	F. Luckman
19249	Do	Ed Lunt
64310	Do	G. Marraty
83599	Do	H. McGinn
71325	Do	A. Meadows

Nominal Roll (Cont'd)

Reg. No	Rank	Name
17076	Driver	A. D. Memory
12926	D°	T. Muller
91782	D°	R. Nolan
12583	D°	R. Osborne
17204	D°	H. Payne
17207	D°	G. Pollard
83245	D°	G. H. Raigan
9130	D°	W. Stevens
12427	D°	Jas Stretle
18454	D°	J. H. Taylor
26070	D°	Geo Thornton
64350	D°	A. Turner
1563	D°	A. S. Webb
13070	D°	H. Watkins
4797	D°	W. Wood

Major, R.F.A.
COMMANDING "A" BTTY. 9TH BDE. R.F.A.

B/87th Brigade
R.F.A.

Nominal Roll of Officers N.C.O.s & Men

	Capt C H Yebay	6764	S.S Weston G.
	Lieut A D Hunter	52300	Sadler Hayes J
	2/Lieut J R Williamson	19145	" Roe J
	2/Lieut C J W York	37343	Fitter Carr J
	2/Lieut J B McCarthy	5787	" Wolstenholme J.
		3261	Gunr Angold J.H.
21121	BSM Garton E.	31940	" Baker C
18156	QMS Hepworth J	1589	" Beale A
35124	Sgt Youle J	89940	" Black W.H
24269	" Hutchinson C	1597	" Bredle W
77877	" Mayow W.J	66793	" Brown S
59309	" Whiterod A	18475	" Bush W.S
39166	For Sgt Green C	9089	" Clark A.W
19257	Cpl Dale H.H.	19263	" Cutland A.J
68087	" Jones G.A	64266	" Cuthbertson J
35778	" Ladis C.W.	13004	" Dunn E
12691	" Webb W.	86068	" Dyer R.S.
61382	Cpl S.S McKenna J	64841	" Farlow A
13224	Bdr Bradley G	66660	" Fildes L
86001	" Glover A.	66391	" Hall A
12597	" Grainger W.C.	13119	" Hanson J
86114	" Hooker S.T	86074	" Harding C
66628	" Hookey G	59190	" Haynes J
18203	" Lee A.E	12804	" Hughes H
13120	" Symonds S	26920	" Hubball J
19837	" Williams H.	19419	" Jackson M.
36499	" Woodburn C.	588114	" Jarvis N.W
92005	A/Bdr Clune J	28860	" Jones C.
92001	" Hilton J	16762	" Joslin J
13900	" Jeffrey J.	85964	" King H.
86786	" Salt J	28732	" Llewellyn H
28983	" Stuart W.A.	59255	" Ludlam J
70954	" Timmins G.H	19174	" Manton C.J.

C/87 Bde., R.F.A.　　　　　7.6.16

Nominal Roll of Officers, Warrant Officers, N.C.O's & Men

Regt. No.	Rank	Name	Regt. No.	Rank	Name
		Officers	42110	A/Bdr.	Wilson, W.
	Capt.	H. N. H. Williamson	78118	"	McGee, R.
	Lieut.	D. Meston	4036	Sergt.	Emery, G. (A.V.C. attached)
	"	R. B. Trollope	43789	Farrier Sgt.	Knight, H.A.
	2nd Lt.	W. E. H. Metcalfe	69591	Cpl. S.S.	Ash, S.
	"	L. Teeling	97519	S.S.	Carnell, H.G.
	"	J. H. Mozley	99003	"	Guppy, E.
			99094	"	Bearham, A.J.
Regt. No.		**W.O.**	12082	"	Geary, A.
24280	B.S.M.	Berryman, E.J.	7362	"	Murray, A.
			89003	Cpl. Saddler	Heal, J.P.
		N.C.O's	97079	Cpl. Wheeler	Daly, O.
86177	Q.M.S.	Hargreaves, F.	18201	Fitter	Sidswell, L.
62316	Sergt.	Crone, E.W.			
744	"	Mitchell, A.			**Men**
4296	"	Smith, R.H.	28698	Gr.	Addicott, L.
45430	"	Harmer, A.R.J.	244	"	Armstrong, J.
60216	"	Playle, E.	6205	"	Anderson, J.
8918	Cpl.	Taylor, S.R.	12993	"	Blackburn, A.
13041	"	Baker, G.	28624	"	Brown, R.
60237	"	Batchelor, A.	24313	"	Burr, H.
37089	"	Gwyer, H.	19903	"	Borkwell, G.
743	Bdr.	Bow, W.	732	"	Beattie, W.
69396	"	Sidswell, J.	12659	"	Bowker, W.
18144	"	Morgan, A.	93597	"	Beckett, G.
13270	"	Duckett, G.	66939	"	Bowen, F.
12085	"	Barlow, J.	74317	"	Brown, J.
13016	"	Fitzmaurice, J.	68770	"	Boorman, A.J.
80416	A/Bdr.	Dover, A.	25123	"	Christopher, G.H.
48506	"	Ryder, J.J.A.	28339	"	Evans, W.
58526	"	Sheppard, H.R.A.	50808	"	Ellis, W.
18780	"	Weaver, W.D.	86553	"	Ensor, A.

52301	Gunr	Midgley S		18703	Driver	Foster R
104541	"	O'Brien J		29022	"	George W
13067	"	Padmore EJ		71655	"	Greenwood H
26058	"	Patterson G		50896	"	Hawes A
45928	"	Philp J		18397	"	Hordacre JJ
92131	"	Pryce G		62469	"	Hawkins A
128864	"	Read G		13126	"	Hatterell WH
16800	"	Robinson HC		12645	"	Heptenstall C
81726	"	Robotham HE		16814	"	Hobbs H
8567	"	Simmonds E		12406	"	Holden W
28361	"	Skinner G		92496	"	Holmes W
86108	"	Smith JJ		12502	"	Hughes J
16968	"	Stacey AE		18147	"	Jennings A
66655	"	Sutton J		12543	"	Jones P
12872	"	Smethurst J		28858	"	Jones CH
1648	"	Tunnicliffe H		13205	"	Kelly P
48571	"	Truss J		19478	"	King HE
37574	"	Waite HK		12525	"	Maybury JJ
12593	"	Wilde R		5970	"	Marks HA
17436	Driver	Abbetts J		36924	"	Moore G
18692	"	Abbott J		37373	"	Morton W
12416	"	Appleton JE		18685	"	McGrath J
13069	"	Barton A		18636	"	McIlroy J
62458	"	Boxall W		13284	"	Ormond A
62643	"	Bridge W		12428	"	Pierce H
18393	"	Bromley J		33471	"	Pinkney HS
86459	"	Buckley S		13109	"	Reed H
92388	"	Campbell W		1099	"	Rex J
18788	"	Clegg J		13059	"	Sealey J
3111	"	Cormack W		97004	"	Taylor James
12657	"	Dalglish A		12353	"	Taylor Jarvis
62628	"	Davies J		12952	"	Toy J
				64250	"	Turner A
86489	"	Duffy J		92068	"	Williams J
13290	"	England S		24588	"	Woof J
81960	"	Evans AS		64253	"	Wright JJ
19936	"	Feltham J				

Regt No.	Rank	Name.	Regt. No	Rank	Name.
841	Gr.	Grieve, J.	12533	Dr.	Booth, J.
12945	"	Garbett, C.	12570	"	Brown, A. J.
18471	"	Gibson, E.	12412	"	Bleazard, H.
35922	"	Gibson, G.	12880	"	Brookes, J.
59068	"	Gettins	13006	"	Byers, H.
6239	"	Harkins, J.	831	"	Bradley, W.J.
36250	"	Horseman, G.R.	71696	"	Bowers, G.A.
24798	"	Hall, J.A.	66461	"	Binns, R.
9287	"	Howell, H.	93596	"	Cook, J.
6244	"	Jackson, J.	654	"	Craig, W.
12830	"	Jackson, J.	702	"	Clunie, W.
26891	"	Kerr, G.	714	"	Christison, J.
12827	"	McGowan, W.	71539	"	Clay, R.
13258	"	Miller, S.	26895	"	Durrant, W.J.
833	"	Minehan, M.	18453	"	Davies
86124	"	Mulhearn, B.	1289	"	Dicker, H.
87695	"	Plumbley, G.	36257	"	Davies, L.J.
15996	"	Pennington, E.	82490	"	Dawson, J.
28622	"	Smith, J.	12408	"	Eccles, W.
48530	"	Smith, C.H.	41765	"	Evanson, H.
70488	"	Smith, J.	12523	"	Fogg, J.
64198	"	Smith, H.	52459	"	Foster, E.
41164	"	Sneddon, W.	91733	"	Gorman, N.
64244	"	Sinclair, J.	772	"	Graham, J.
64398	"	Secker, W.	18707	"	Gildrist, M.
76057	"	Simons, G.	76247	"	Green, J.C.
18213	"	Weller, W.H.	83312	"	Harrison, E.
25757	"	Wiles, C.E.	12977	"	Hardy, E.
81467	"	Gibbs, C.	18455	"	Higson, A.
6237	Dr.	Anderson, W.	13203	"	Hughes, C.H.
6238	"	Borland, W	18138	"	Hewins, J.
12943	"	Bridgeman, G.	12582	"	Hamilton, W.

Regt No.	Rank	Name			
12600	Dr.	Hainey, W			
6242	"	Harkins, E.			
8568	"	Herrington, FW			
13955	"	Hendriksen, G.			
29062	"	Jones, E.			
61739	"	Knott, P.O.			
761	"	Lewis, F.			
13010	"	Marsden, W.			
66150	"	Moore, M.			
13262	"	Merrick			
64390	"	Middleton, W.J.			
12808	"	Newton, J.			
14367	"	Pinnell, W.			
13041	"	Padfield, D.			
1839	"	Russell, W.			
71492	"	Rainford, E.			
71432	"	Read, J.J.			
1577	"	Stay, J.H.			
71583	"	Skane, B.W.			
16967	"	Smart, A.			
48568	"	Tootill, A.			
10742	"	Yates, H.			

L/Tuling 4th d/87 RH
to O.C.

Regt No.	Rank	Name			

NOMINAL ROLL
OF
OFFICERS, W.O.s N.C.O.s & MEN D/87th F.A. Bde.

Rank	Reg'tl No.	Name
Capt	H	Russell
Lieut	E	Cruickshank
Lieut	J.F.	Mayne
2Lieut	E	Jones
2Lieut	G.C.Doct	Du Vallon

Rank	Reg'tl No.	Name
W.O. Class 2	10898	BSM Lowe W.

Rank	No	Name
BQMS	30022	Trim A.G.
Sgt	43442	Nevett B.J.
"	8610	Jefferek W.L.
"	8609	Howard R
"	63988	Perrett H
"	69216	Bowson J.H.
Cpls	29289	Clarke A.H.
	28645	Walters E.J.S.
	36646	Gladwin W.E.
	6680	McDonald T
	13183	Dersley H
Bs	18429	Fitzpatrick J
	36952	Cain F.H.
	34329	Burdett H
	36646	Henshall S.
	13247	Weeks F
	38384	Griffiths D
	3660	Ruck G.
	13206	Mannings V.A.
C/Br	832	Deary J.
	82455	Winstanley J
	19086	Clarke J
	16485	Bullock L
	94349	McConnell J
	12354	Graynor J

ARTIFICERS

Reg'tl No	Rank	Name
88855	FarSgt	Steele J
12994	S/S	Pusey J
86414	L/	Gillingham T
13164		Phillips R
80319	F/S	Dumant W
8613	Whr	Jones T.L.
101454	Sadr	Hammon E
75250	"	Veasey C.

Gunners

No	Name
34381	Aldag H
1255	Atkinson F
36665	Boulton H
95962	Barker G.H.
36909	Brabender C
34363	Cottle R
34244	Chubb A.W.
12314	Corbett J.
8639	Chapman E
98262	Carstairs A
29620	Evans A
15421	Faulkner C
95101	74 A
18664	Grace L
106408	Gibson A.W.
11024	Gregson W
106366	Gurling E
58730	Hurnell T.H.G
8666	Hitchon S.
34360	Jones N.
20041	Jones J.R.
73693	Lomax F.W.
34063	Longden J
6660	McClaren R.A.
13140	McIntyre G
13184	Maidment H
95585	McHugh J
64189	Murray E.B.
13050	Mafeld F
634	Portous A
12955	Powell E
74268	Puggott D
94465	Prussey W.T.
14293	Parr H.W.
29205	Payne A.J.
29184	Short W

GUNNERS

No	Name
83200	Symonds V.R.
12980	Stephenson G.
103373	Stoddart J
25935	Tams L
13161	Taylor A
43636	Tibbett H
94959	Twiggs F.D.
36269	Thompson J.R
62455	Wilson F
29069	Wolfe G.W.
28912	Wood A
6293	Ward J.
62938	Wright E
102938	Vygus W

DRIVERS

No	Name
12688	Buster H
46063	Barter G
12546	Bradwell P.H.
19264	Baker W
5697	Butland T
36529	Bancroft H
36526	Burton E
46010	Brooker W.G
5218	Cudlip T
4943	Crowhurst T.W.
52449	Dickson T
19241	Eyers A.E.
64214	Froggatt
106383	Fisher J
38402	Green C
50858	Garrard C
46009	Heard R
12429	Kilshaw G.
12861	Jones J
12945	Lauder W
82366	Leese J.S.
12569	Morris M.
5454	Nadin W
12588	Nelson F
406	Polhan L
13005	Parry J.C.
6336	Reilly R
36363	Revell R.S.
36362	Revell W.T.
83148	Rafferty L
6240	Ramsay W
19368	Robinson J.J.
25949	Swarbuck J
82375	Smith S
12829	Smith T
	Smith Ech.
28864	Shields C
403	Staley J.B
13050	Spicer W
5590	

DRIVERS

No	Name
12998	Townsend G
5088	Thompson J
13195	Wright F.T
12942	Wardle A
24154	Walker W
13103	Walsh F
6224	Wilson W
46184	Wynne R
82540	Yeoman H

Attached from A.V.C.
964 Sgt Richardson F.

From 6th Wors. Res.
11830 Pte Clarke G.F.

J.F. Mayne Lt R.F.A
Commanding "D" Battery 87th Brigade R.F.A

7 JUN 1916

Nominal Roll – W/19 Hy. T. M. Battery.

Reg No.	Rank and Name		Reg No.	Rank and Name	
	Captain	Shattock. A. Comdg	64330	Gr.	Ibbotson. J.
	2/Lieut.	Barfoot. W.	18276	"	Jackson. T.
29155	a/B.S.M.	Old. J. A.	32500	"	Jones. W. P.
963	Sgt.	Sanderson. J. C.	12147	"	Jones. R. G.
83415	"	Anderson. S.	91817	"	Marshall. A.
50799	Cpl.	Eales. F. W.	10072	"	McHenry.
45946	"	Ryan.	18281	"	McGlin.
61912	"	Smith. A. T.	100469	"	Mayo. W.
69780	"	Taylor. G. J.	1163	"	Pallett. E. A.
11420	Bor.	Langford. A. H.	83580	"	Read. W.
95114	"	Stevens. J. B.	57390	"	Riorden. G. D.
4002	"	Steele. S. J.	5712	"	Riley. W. B.
29502	"	Stanford. J.	117105	"	Stephenson. J. W.
47572	a/Bor.	Lawrence. S. D.	66292	"	Stevens. F. W.
77592	"	Winstone. A. J.	102024	"	Seward. H. G.
57237	Gr.	Adams. N.	122819	"	Spencer. F. J.
795	"	Bell. P.	66151	"	Tinkler. A. F.
129234	"	Birch. L.	104133	"	Todd.
75975	"	Brotherwood. H.	19754	"	Tyer.
12956	"	Bradley. J.	5090	"	Walsh. J.
46328	"	Briars. E. J.	58249	"	Wilson W. G.
45934	"	Christie. D.	92128	"	Williams. T.
109141	"	Clark. G.	96572	"	Whelan. W.
92429	Dr.	Dean. B.	12868	"	Mullineux. H.
80893	Gr.	Donlin. E.	34012	"	Young. W. L.
64173	"	Denton. J.	18161	Fitter	Smith. G.
57073	"	Dowling.			
10069	"	Evans.			
50202	"	Eaton.			
38166	"	Farthing. W.			
7391	"	Foster. J. G.			
109442	"	French. L. T.			
49292	"	Furlong. D.			
50864	"	Garrod. J. G.			
17434	Dr.	Gibbons. R. H.			
25257	Gr.	Godfrey. T.			
64381	"	Harrison. A.			
103742	"	Harra. J.			
116326	"	Heald. J. W.			

Mc Adie
87th FA Bde

Herewith Nominal Roll W/19 Heavy Trench Mortar Battery, up to date.
9.6.16.

A. Shattock Lieut RFA
Comdg W/19 H.T.M. Bty

Army Form C. 2118.

WAR DIARY
or
INTELLIGENCE SUMMARY.
(Erase heading not required.)

Instructions regarding War Diaries and Intelligence Summaries are contained in F. S. Regs., Part II. and the Staff Manual respectively. Title pages will be prepared in manuscript.

Place	Date	Hour	Summary of Events and Information	Remarks and references to Appendices
THEROUANNE	1.		Brigade Training with 57th Infantry Brigade on Training Area, 4/18th. Batteries and 1 How: Battery (C/89). Bavincuette 24.81.	
"	2.		Brigade training with 57th Infantry Brigade on Training Area. It started to rain heavily at 3.30 P.M., which somewhat interfered with the success of the operations. Owing to ammunition being wet through the major general did not hold a Powwow at the close of the 6 phenomena. Bavincuette 24.70.	
"	3.		The Batteries did not turn out today; the men needed a day's rest after a somewhat strenuous week on the Training Area. Weather still continues fine. It was cloudy in the morning and looked like rain, but by mid-day the sun came out. Bavincuette 24.66.	
"	4.		Divisional Training under R.O.C. 19th Division. Bavincuette 24.41. The Brigade went out on a Night-Scheme at 12 mid day returned to billets at 5 P.M. after the conclusion of Divisional Training.	

2353 Wt. W2541/1454 700,000 5/15 D. D. & L. A.D.S.S./Forms/C. 2118.

Army Form C. 2118.

WAR DIARY
or
INTELLIGENCE SUMMARY.
(Erase heading not required.)

Instructions regarding War Diaries and Intelligence Summaries are contained in F. S. Regs., Part II. and the Staff Manual respectively. Title pages will be prepared in manuscript.

Place	Date	Hour	Summary of Events and Information	Remarks and references to Appendices
	May			
THEROUANNE	5		Divisional Training under G.O.C. 14th Division. Battery staff only now taken out. Baromatic 29.19.	
	6		Batteries at disposal of Battery Commanders. Baromatic 29.45.	
BELLOY-SUR-SOMME.	7		Riding party consisting of 1 N.C.O. per Battery & R.A.C., under Orderley Officer left Pour BERGUETTE at 9.10 a.m., arriving LONGEAU at 5 p.m. A motor lorry took the party to its billeting area.	
"	9 #		H.Q, 87th Bde, D/87, & 14 R.A.C., arrived LONGEAU at 6.45 a.m., and proceeded to billeting area B/87, arrived LONGEAU at 10 a.m., and to R.A.C. C/87 & 14 R.A.C. arrived at 7.30 P.M. D/87 & 14 R.A.C. at 10.30 P.M.	
"	10		Batteries busy settling down & making the best & have been comfortable. AMIENS is out of bounds to all ranks below major general, except on very special cases.	

Army Form C. 2118.

WAR DIARY
or
INTELLIGENCE SUMMARY.
(Erase heading not required.)

Instructions regarding War Diaries and Intelligence Summaries are contained in F. S. Regs., Part II. and the Staff Manual respectively. Title pages will be prepared in manuscript.

Place	Date	Hour	Summary of Events and Information	Remarks and references to Appendices
Dellnoy-Sur-Somme	11		Weather cool and dull.	
"	12		Col. Dennistoun saw C.R.A. 34 Div. and reconnoitered positions for Batteries in the vicinity of ALBERT.	
"	13		Battery commanders under Col. Dennistoun proceeded to ALBERT and selected positions for their batteries and made arrangements for a material and working parties.	
"	14		The Chaplain held a service at 10.4 am in the Bompards. Battery commanders fetched horses from the B.A.C., and got rid of their foor horses. Major Cavendish went on leave.	
"	15		Very wet morning but cleared up at mid-day. Working parties of 20 men per Battery proceeded to ALBERT to construct positions they will be relieved by the Batteries of the 34th Div. to which they are attached.	

Army Form C. 2118.

WAR DIARY
or
INTELLIGENCE SUMMARY.
(Erase heading not required.)

Instructions regarding War Diaries and Intelligence Summaries are contained in F. S. Regs., Part II. and the Staff Manual respectively. Title pages will be prepared in manuscript.

Place	Date	Hour	Summary of Events and Information	Remarks and references to Appendices
	May			
Bellacourt-Souastre	16th		Colonel Dennistoun proceeded on leave to England and Major Longstreet took over command of the Brigade.	
"	17th to 21st		Battery Commanders reports work progressing satisfactorily on positions in Forward Area, and that plenty of material is available. The weather is abnormally fine.	
"	27th to 31st		Work on gun pits in the Forward Area is progressing satisfactorily. PL Props have been cut and sent up in motor lorries.	

2333 Wt. W2544/1454 700,000 5/15 D. D. & L. A.D.S.S./Forms/C. 2118.

WAR DIARY or INTELLIGENCE SUMMARY

Army Form C. 2118

89th RFA Brigade. 19/JUNE VOL II

Place	Date	Hour	Summary of Events and Information	Remarks and references to Appendices
BELLOY-SUR-SOMME.	June 1st to 6th		Work is going on much in the groundwork area - pit props are being cut and sent up daily. There has been a considerable amount of hostile shelling during the past few days, and a number of shells of all calibres have fallen in and about ALBERT.	
	7th to 12th		The work in the forward area continues with success. Colonel D. envisions receives orders for the general offensive and commences same to Battery Commanders.	
	12th to 16th		Weather remains overcast but improves.	
	17th		Brigade moves to D.22.d and goes into bivouac lines in the open.	
	19th		Communication complete for the Somme offensive.	
	20th		Battery groups complete in readiness for general offensive.	

WAR DIARY
or
INTELLIGENCE SUMMARY

Army Form C. 2118

Place	Date	Hour	Summary of Events and Information	Remarks and references to Appendices
BUIRE 10th/623rd			Advanced positions for wagon line reconnoitred at E/10.b. Forward routes reconnoitred and signal wire dumps at forward Brigade head quarters.	
	24th		Bombardment of front line lines by 18 pdr of 34th Division observed. NEUGOLAND area wire were cut.	
	25th		Bombardment continues POZIERES CONTALMAISON and MAMETZ severely damaged.	
	26th		Bombardment continues the Second line parapet damaged and wire cut.	
	27th		Brigade finally disposed for General Offensive Liaison Officers. LIEUT E WILSON-HUGHES with 12th Divl Arty with OP at S7d 89 LIEUT C.W. TO R.R. with	

Army Form C. 2118

WAR DIARY
or
INTELLIGENCE SUMMARY

(Erase heading not required.)

Instructions regarding War Diaries and Intelligence Summaries are contained in F. S. Regs., Part II. and the Staff Manual respectively. Title Pages will be prepared in manuscript.

Place	Date	Hour	Summary of Events and Information	Remarks and references to Appendices
BUIRE	28		Batt N.F. LIEUT J. WAYNE with 55th Batt N.F. "y" day. Two batteries 28 hours bombardment on whole front.	
	29		"y" day continues. Heavy and 18-pr bombardment on whole front.	
TARA	30		"y" day. Brigade moved into action on slopes of TARA - USNA HILL. Brigade Headquarters at W.30 d 6.89. with the intention of called by name) FORWARD GROUP 34th Div. C/88	

19th Div.
III.Corps.

Headquarters.

87th BRIGADE. R.F.A.

J U L Y

1 9 1 6

WAR DIARY
INTELLIGENCE SUMMARY

87 Bde. R.F.A. Army Form C. 2118
1st July Vol 12

BATTLE OF THE SOMME.

Place	Date	Hour	Summary of Events and Information	Remarks and references to Appendices
TARA.	July 1st	7.30	87th Bde in observation received launched against LA BOISELLE. HEUGOLAND ROUND WOOD. 87th J.O. Bde. attached to 103RD INF Bde. BRIG-GEN CAMERON) 101st Bde moves in the wake of 21st Division man night pushing were up the slopes towards QUADRANGLE TRENCH. without being held up by hostile fire.	
		7.45	Royal Scots reported charging past SCOTS REDOUBT	
		10.30	Definitely ascertained that 102nd Brigade has twice against LA BOISELLE on the 8th against MILLERS	
		2 pm	19th Division moving up into the field.	
		6 pm	19th Division owing to shortage of time allotted for	
		6.15 pm	before coming up. LA BOISELLE Division to come up into the fire LT. C.J.W. Gov. wounded	

WAR DIARY
or
INTELLIGENCE SUMMARY

Army Form C. 211

BATTLE OF THE SOMME

Place	Date	Hour	Summary of Events and Information	Remarks and references to Appendices
TARA	July 2	PM 3	Intense bombardment of OVILLERS synchronous with advance on LA BOISSELLE by 58th Bde	
	3	4pm	Captures of the greater part of the village	
	4		after m HORSE-SHOE trench and further advance in remainder of OVILLERS by bomber	
	5		21st Division established in QUADRANGLE TRENCH.	
	6	8pm	River m CONTALMAISON successful. Enemy	
	7		River m CONTALMAISON successful in a N.E. direction and	
	8		engaged & his turning infantry in the open	
			Consolidate his inflict on infantry continuation.	
	9	4pm	German counter attack in POZIERES	
			completely stopped by our artillery fire	
	14		attack on POZIERES by 111th Inf/Bde supported	
	15		by 87 Bde. Regt of Barley	
			Artillery joined to make the infantry	
			for 7th Div. now endeavy	

Army Form C. 21

WAR DIARY
or
INTELLIGENCE SUMMARY
(Erase heading not required.)

Instructions regarding War Diaries and Intelligence Summaries are contained in F.S. Regs., Part II. and the Staff Manual respectively. Title Pages will be prepared in manuscript.

Place	Date	Hour	Summary of Events and Information	Remarks and references to Appendices
POZIÈRES	Sept 4/9/16		BATTLE OF THE SOMME. Reconnoitred in attack E of OVILLERS. 2/LT S. N. Humphreys wounded then trying to amend Thy continuous rifle LIAISON with LOYAL NORTH LANCS. 3rd LANCS (LT-COL WINDSOR) then with LOYAL NORTH LANCS (LT-COL MARYAT)	
	20 Sept		Relief complete 78th Bde by 2nd Bde. RBs at Australian Division (LT-COL BROWN)	

WAR DIARY
or
INTELLIGENCE SUMMARY

Army Form C. 211

(Erase heading not required.)

BATTLE of SOMME. (con.)

Place	Date	Hour	Summary of Events and Information	Remarks and references to Appendices
TARA REDOUBT	20.	9 AM	Colonel Dennistoun reconnoitred position to engage SWITCH LINE meeting BRIG-GEN MONKHOUSE at 9.30 am at 86TH F.A. Bde Head Quarters in SAUSAGE VALLEY. Afterwards Col Dennistoun appointed to meet his Battery Commanders at F.4. c.66. to carry the reconnaissance further.	
		12.30 P14	This was done and batteries were withdrawn	
		to 4.	from TARA and came into action the same	
		afternoon on the northern slope of CATERPILLAR		
		5 to 8	VALLEY. in S.21.a with Head Quarters at MARLBORO WOOD.	
		7.30.	Violent. Air fight in which one German was shot to earth with no loss to ourselves.	
		4 p.m.	Six German aeroplanes flew over battery.	

Army Form C. 2118

WAR DIARY
or
INTELLIGENCE SUMMARY
(Erase heading not required.)

Place	Date	Hour	Summary of Events and Information	Remarks and references to Appendices
TARA	20		Position making a further reconnaissance of our new positions. Capt. H.N.H. Williamson sent forward to which has forward for 19th Brigade.	
		4 to 7 pm	"B" Aux, "B" Balloon observed the congestion of men, vehicles and horse in the Valley leading N.W. from FRICOURT. Troublesome aircraft on the morrow.	
	21	9 AM	LIAISON established with BRIG GEN ONSLOW commanding 57th Inf Bde with Headquarters at S/4.b.41. LIEUT WILSON-HUGHES appointed LIAISON OFFICER.	
	12 noon		Batteries in position as follows A87 Church MARTINPUICH. B87 Sixteen Lin. 32b C87 Do Do D87 NW corner HIGHWOOD.	

WAR DIARY
or
INTELLIGENCE SUMMARY

(Erase heading not required.)

Army Form C. 2118

Place	Date	Hour	Summary of Events and Information	Remarks and references to Appendices
MRL BORO WOOD	22	10.55 pm	Orders issued to Battn. to spares area M 32 c & D until the importation for injured armour to be carried out by 57th Inf Bde.	
		2.5 am	Battalion LIAISON officer reports in armour at S 8 b 2 5 in BAZENTIN-LE-PETIT.	
		4.12	Report receives that German Barrage directed on BAZENTIN LE GRAND Valley.	
		6	Orders received to deepen SWITCH LINE portion allotted 89th Inf Bde S 3 C 40.65 to S 2 d 65.65.	
		6.3	Shortly after message receives to begin its further own.	
		6.30	Watches synchronized at BECOURT CHATEAU by III Corps. Staff officer. Battn. heavily shelled by (a) 5.9" (b) 4"2" (6) 8" 11 casualties reported in the Barrage	

Place	Date	Hour	Summary of Events and Information	Remarks and references to Appendices
MARLBORO WOOD	23 Aug		Attack on SWITCH LINE failed for two reasons. (a) Two Horse Arty. between Corps were at variance as much as one hour. Jno. batteries not coordinated between Corps. Casualties were heavy and a/c to attack the line ran 10th Warwicks S8658 to S8C44 from which trench ran S9a33 abcin trench running from S3C02 to S9a28.	S.L.L.
		11.15	Line in front of SWITCH LINE to be left when Batteries did not suffer so much from hostile shelling. O CATERPILLAR Valley.	
		P.M.	M.G. Emplacements reported at S3C65. S3C75 and S3C85.	
		10.15	Orders received to prevent repair of wire in front of SWITCH LINE north 4.5" How. and prevent enemy's trenches north 18-pr. howitzers in enfilade Batteries	

WAR DIARY
or
INTELLIGENCE SUMMARY

Army Form C. 2118

Place	Date	Hour	Summary of Events and Information	Remarks and references to Appendices
MARLBORO WOOD	23	PM 10.15	B. cony.	See
	24	AM 6	Heavy shelling of CATERPILLAR VALLEY took place at 6, 6.50 and 7.20. Whole area specialia attention being paid to the Maltars' Wood road at (one shell dropped at MONTAU BAN) of extremely large calibre. The battery of the 25-TH Bde. manoeuvred in front and in rear head earrielai. by trenches blown in but no casualties were reported in the Brigade.	
		PM 5.22	Report sent to Div. Artz. that continued intermittent shelling of CATERPILLAR VALLEY throughout the day had the result of blowing up a Bomb Store situated at western edge of CATERPILLAR WOOD. Very Light went up in this explosion. LIAISON officer Mlorits BAZENTIN-LE-PETIT shells as 30 pm.	821.

WAR DIARY or INTELLIGENCE SUMMARY

Army Form C. 2118

Place	Date	Hour	Summary of Events and Information	Remarks and references to Appendices
MARLBORO WOOD	24	AM	Liaison officer reports that on night of 23/24 R.W.F's relieved WARWICKS; the WILTS the N LANCS; the WELCH the GLOUCESTERS. Heir return there is no gap in line between HIGH WOOD and WINDMILL. CAPT H H WILLIAMSON returns to Bn in his was bequias Bn Headquarters.	B.Ms.
	25	AM 10.30	Heavy shelling of CATERPILLAR VALLEY continues without abrear till 7 pm starting from the eastern end. 86th BpBde suffered COL AE WILSON being reported wounded, visited this area and mentally BRIG-GEN. MONKHOUSE saw refuge in old German funnel W of MKPE BoRo' WOOD. B/67 mOr being heavily shelled remained in position.	
		12.50	86th F A Brigade HD officers turn up position close by 87th Bde Headquarters	

WAR DIARY or INTELLIGENCE SUMMARY

Army Form C. 2118

Place	Date	Hour	Summary of Events and Information	Remarks and references to Appendices
MARLBORO' WOOD.	26	10.10 AM	Line newly formed by Scimen will henceforward be called INTERMEDIATE LINE.	R.L.n
		3 PM to 7	Heavy artillery bombardment S2c84 to S3c85 Field Gun paid attention to trench S2c84 - S2c62 Quiet day	
		4.10	LOOP trench reported constructed near FOUR TREES S2d102.	
		6.30	Reported to Div. arty registration successfully carried out	
		9.20	Red and Green rockets going up SW of MARTINPUICH	R.L.n
	27	AM 7.30 to 10	Heavy bombardment of MARLBORO ROAD. Reported to Divl. Arty. that fan shells fell all through the night. Lt WILLIAMSON B/87 wounded in the bear by shrapnel MAJOR A. DRYSDALE went to reconnoitre INTERMEDIATE LINE and reported missing believed killed. Biographies not alway in Summary	

WAR DIARY
or
INTELLIGENCE SUMMARY

(Erase heading not required.)

Army Form C. 2118

Place	Date	Hour	Summary of Events and Information	Remarks and references to Appendices
MARLBORO' WOOD	27	4.50 pm	Reported capture of portion of LONGUEVAL by XV Corps	S.Ell.
	28	am 10	Reported all quiet during the night both in front and with Tortoise. Hopkins of Major Drysdale	
		4 pm	Capt A.B. Sweet-Escott appointed to command A Sqn vice Major A.I. DRYSDALE missing believed killed	
		10 pm	Reported counter attack on LONGUEVAL	
	29	am 12.30	Patrols sent out to reconnoitre INTERMEDIATE LINE found Germans lying in front of their front line. Our party immediately commenced and enabled patrols to return safely	S.L.W.
		1.30		
		-5	All quiet on all fronts.	

Army Form C. 2118

WAR DIARY
or
INTELLIGENCE SUMMARY
(Erase heading not required.)

Instructions regarding War Diaries and Intelligence Summaries are contained in F.S. Regs., Part II. and the Staff Manual respectively. Title Pages will be prepared in manuscript.

Place	Date	Hour	Summary of Events and Information	Remarks and references to Appendices
MARLBORO' WOOD	29 Aug	11.30	Sent. went. a/tom Aferically telld. off to firing at M 22 d 25 on receipt of the word "ALBERT".	folls.
		PM 12.30	3. Hun aeroplane over bombing garrison, with 8 of ours.	
		2.15	Heavy enemy shelling of CATERPILLAR VALLEY. commenced. 8" Being shelled with 5.9" and lyddite calibre. Also two 6" gun 10ph batts very heavy. There is ammunition dump working. from a most worrying shelling is coming in direction on line LE SARS - COURCELETTE Shelling stopped 2.40 pm	J. U.
		3.6 3.30	Brigad bombarded SWITCH LINE and INTERMEDIATE LINE. Occasional rounds of heavy arty in CATERPILLAR VALLEY.	

1875. Wt. W593/826 1,000,000 4/15 J.B.C. & A. A.D.S.S./Forms/C. 2118.

Army Form C. 2118

WAR DIARY
or
INTELLIGENCE SUMMARY
(Erase heading not required.)

Place	Date	Hour	Summary of Events and Information	Remarks and references to Appendices
MAMETZ WOOD	30 29	10.15	Quiet delivery, in remnants of LONGUEVAL. Barrages SWITCH LINE for a quarter of an hour.	
		10.30	19th Divl. Operation Order for 30th July received. All reports quiet on our front. Quiet aerial activity throughout the day.	Ltr
	30	AM 1 to 10 P.M.	Intermittent shelling of CATERPILLAR VALLEY. Orders issued for the attack to commence 6.10 pm 30th July from direction of MAMETZ WOOD. 2 carrier pigeons flew across at BAZENTIN-LE-PETIT. towards German lines.	
		4.0	INTERMEDIATE LINE began bombardment of German to right and left of the Brigade by Divisions.	Ltr
		4.50	Relieved by Regts. own and warning wanted in the capture of German strong points on the HIGH WOOD. 13 ways. Reports by BAZENTIN-LE-PETIT road in the morning and counter-attack. Artillery till 7 AM. to recapture strong points. Directed by the enemy failure.	

Army Form C. 2118.

WAR DIARY
or
INTELLIGENCE SUMMARY.
(Erase heading not required.)

Place	Date	Hour	Summary of Events and Information	Remarks and references to Appendices
MARLBORO WOOD	31	7 AM.	Infantry retired down in trenches having slung Brisk rifle fire.	RLh
		9 PM	Bombardment going on on right air grids in front	RLh
			BIOGRAPHICAL NOTE on MAJOR A. I. DRYSDALE R.G.A. (attached R.F.A.)	
			MAJOR ALEXANDER ICELEY DRYSDALE received commission in the ROYAL GARRISON ARTILLERY in MARCH 1900 and served 7 years in MAURITIUS first as an A.D.C. then as military secretary to the Governor MAURITIUS (Sir COURTNEY-BOYLE)	RLh

2353. Wt. W2544/1454 700,000 5/15 D. D. & L. A.D.S.S./Forms/C. 2118.

Army Form C. 2118.

WAR DIARY
or
INTELLIGENCE SUMMARY.
(Erase heading not required.)

3 year tour at GIBRALTER followed by the
Ordnance College, from him Further
outbreak of war, in the GARRISON. I SPIKE ISLAND. He
was posted to the 19th Divl Arty on transfer to RFA
and command No 3 Section DAC. The nine months
on Jan 15 1915 he was appointed to command
MR3 which appointment he held, till hereto reported
"siding" on July 27th 1916.
Promotion to Major took
place on March 16.1

Lieut RFA
F. F. Chilver LCOL
cmsg 87th 7ABr
1/8/16

19th Divisional Artillery.

87th BRIGADE

ROYAL FIELD ARTILLERY

AUGUST 1 9 1 6 :::::

Army Form C. 2118.

VOL 13

WAR DIARY
INTELLIGENCE SUMMARY.
(Erase heading not required.)

Place	Date	Hour	Summary of Events and Information	Remarks and references to Appendices
Marlbro' Wood	1/8		Informed that our relief by the 15th Divisional Artillery on the nights 3/4 and 4/5. A reconnoitring party of the 71st Brigade Royal Field Artillery arrived while our Headquarters was being heavily shelled with 8" Armour Piercing Shell. They proceeded to inspect the dugouts in particular that which had been struck by an 8" A-P Shell without suffering any harm. The lines of fire wereshown and the general system of our communications.	F.L.W.
do	4/8		A section of each battery relieved by: one of the corresponding batteries of th e 71st F.A.Brigade.	F.L.W.
BECOURT	5/8		Relief reported complete at 6 am Our Headquarters removed to the wagon line in rear of BECOURT WOOD . Starting at 9.0 am from thee wagon lines, each battery moved independently into rest billets at BEAU-COURT	F.L.W.
BEAUCOURT	6/8		At 6.10 pm the brigade was inspected and complimented by Lieut-Gen. Sir James Pulteney Commanding III Corps	F.L.W.
SALEUX	7/8		Batteries entrained at LONGEAUX Brigade Headquarters at SALEUX. Thetrain journey was effected without mishap or casualty – Batteries detrained at GODEWAERSVELDE and Brigade Headquarters at STEENBECQUE . The Brigade went into billets at STEENVOORDE spending the night 7/8 there.	F.L.W.
STEENVOORDE	8/8		One section of each battery relieved one section of the corresponding battery of the 251st Brigade 50th Div. in theSector YPRES-WARTS- MESSINES	F.L.W.
KEMMEL SHELTERS	9/8	12 noon 9th August	Relief of the 251st Field Artillery Brigade Complete by Positionsof Unitsas follows :- 87th F.A.Brigade Headquarters KEMMEL SHELTERS A/87 Adjoining SIEGE FARM B/87 Adjoining KEMMEL Military cemetery C/87 North of PLOEGSTEERT (to emf ilade SPANBROEKMOLEN SALIENT) D/87 In rear ofLINDENHOEK	

Army Form C. 2118.

WAR DIARY
or
INTELLIGENCE SUMMARY.

(Erase heading not required.)

Place	Date	Hour	Summary of Events and Information	Remarks and references to Appendices
KEMMEL SHELTERS	9/8			
	9/8 to 17/8		"CENTRE GROUP" = 19th Divl. Artillery and included in addition to its own batteries B/89 situated at LINDENHOEK. The chief feature of our early observations was the distinct daily bombardment of our front line trenches by hostile Trench Mortars. This was no regular as to almost form a regular routine under the direct control of Corps. Buried DW was the order of the day with satisfactory results up to the present. In the period upto the 17th August three organised shoots were taken part in by this Group. Artillery (1) Firing in conjunction with V Corps Heavy. This was carried out with observed effect. (2) On the 15th August Bombardment of SPANBROEKMOLEN by "D" Howitzers took place. The enemy retaliated feebly on our front line to which swift punishment was meted out by the Group's opening fire on both flanks of SPANBROEKMOLEN SALIENT. (3) On 17th August in conjunction with H.T.Ms. suspected enemy O.Ps were bombarded. Observation for effect is difficult but the retaliation the enemy showed, indicated much annoyance. Spasmodic hostile T.M.activity was reported during this period. Firing in conjunction with aeroplanes took place on four occasions, on three of which the target was reached.	S.L.v.
	17/8 to 24/8		During this period our aeroplane shoots were fair, having fired on two occasions. No outstanding feature reported	S.L.v.

Army Form C. 2118.

WAR DIARY
or
INTELLIGENCE SUMMARY.
(Erase heading not required.)

Instructions regarding War Diaries and Intelligence Summaries are contained in F. S. Regs., Part II. and the Staff Manual respectively. Title pages will be prepared in manuscript.

Place	Date	Hour	Summary of Events and Information	Remarks and references to Appendices
KEMMEL SHELTERS	17/8 to 24/8 (cont)		Enemy's artillery was particularly quiet during this period. On 22nd August, the Flash of an Anti-Aircraft Gunwas seen west end of wood about O 25 d 5 50 Visibility poor therefore exact location impossible Movement was seen repeatedly seen in houses and trees notably at N.24.d.3½.1 An organised shoot on the 19th inst. drew re some retaliation on our front and support line trenches. During the 21st August several opportunities were offered of checking movement seen in enemy lines, though no retaliation is reported to have resulted. On August 22nd clouds of dense black smoke were observed rising from COMINES Station continuing for about an hour A Carrier Pigeon rose from where the WYTSCHAETE - KEMMEL road crosses the enemy line Prevailing wind during this period was S.W.(except N.W. on August 22nd)	F.L.W.
	25/8		A deal of new work observed at N.30.a.2.5.5 (app) and signalling with Flapper was seen there also.	S.L.W.
	26/8		Hostile activity considerably increased today owing to the clear atmosphere affording good observation. Our reply effectively countered this enemy activity.	
	27/8		HELL FARM N.W. of MESSINES was observed on fire. Carrier pigeons rose from this place at 1.0 pm and crossed in the direction of KEMMEL	F.L.W.
	28/8		A battery position suspected at HUNS FARM and registration	

WAR DIARY
or
INTELLIGENCE SUMMARY.

(Erase heading not required.)

Army Form C. 2118.

Place	Date	Hour	Summary of Events and Information	Remarks and references to Appendices
KEMMEL SHELTERS	29/8		registration was carried out accordingly.	G.Lv.
	30/8		Registration on road junction N.E. of WYTSCHAETE was carried out Visibility very poor indeed more especially during and after the thunderstorm which came and went till late afternoon. Rain fell in astonishing torrents testing earthworks of all kinds Roads ceased to exist, and trenches and dugouts became untenable Scheme for the night 29/30 was cancelled. Rain continued to fall heavily during the night, and daylight did not bring a slackening. Instead a heavy gale blew, and all day the front line trenches were not visible	G.Lv.
	31/8		Scheme which was arranged for the night 29thh/30th was partially carried by the 23rd and 36th Divisions. The raid disclosed some dead Germans in the front line trenches. The scheme was a successful one. On our immediate front the unfavourable state of the weather prevented the pre-arranged scheme substantiating.	
	31/8		The weather has altogether changed with a rapidly rising barometer. An air-fight was witnessed in the morning about 7.30 am with successful issue for our airmen. END OF MONTHLY INTELLIGENCE SUMMARY.	

WAR DIARY of 87th Brigade R.F.A.
or
INTELLIGENCE SUMMARY

Army Form C. 2118.

September vol 14

Place	Date	Hour	Summary of Events and Information	Remarks and references to Appendices
KEMMEL	SEPTEMBER 1915			
	1		Position of A/87 was shelled from 9.30 AM to 3.0 PM at intervals. Activity of hostile artillery wasmarked.	
	2		Minenwerfer activity on Front Line on G1 and G2 Sectors. 77mm. fired on our whole front apparently from SPANBROEKMOLEN Salient	
	3		Gas Alarm was ON all day. A/87 position was again shelled with 5.9" Howitzer shells. One direct hit was obtained on gun-pit wounding five of the detachment. 2.30 PM 2nd	
	4		Determined aggression was maintained by our artillery on enemy's front system and battery positions	
	5		Visibility was very bad all day and next to no firing was done by either side. Much train traffic was seen though between WERVICQ and COMINES the smoke of five trains being seen within a comparatively short space of time.	
	6		This day was marked by an increased activity on our part and a corresponding decrease on that of the enemy. Observation Posts and rearward positions received the most attention on our part. A screen located at D.1.a d.3.2. being effectively shelled.	
	7		Relief of one section per battery was reported complete. The usual aggressive activity was continued thereby considerably concealing the relief.	
	8		Relief of 87th F.A Brigade complete by a Brigade of the 4th Canadian Divisional Artillery. Brigade moved to rest billets at METEREN with Brigade Headquarters in BAILLEUL. Reorganisation from 4-gun to 6-gun batteries effected on this day.	

WAR DIARY
or
INTELLIGENCE SUMMARY

(Erase heading not required.)

Army Form C. 2118.

Place	Date	Hour	Summary of Events and Information	Remarks and references to Appendices
KEMMEL T13 c 4 2	9		87th F A Brigade moved up into the sector of PLOEGSTEERT composed as follows occupying positions indicated :- A/87 F A Brigade (Captain J W T Newberry) U 25 a 6. 2½ B/87 F A Brigade (Captain C H Tebay) T 24 d 4. 4 C/87 F A Brigade (Captain H N H Williamson) T 17 b 6 1½ D/87 F A Brigade (Captain H Russell) U 19 a 5 5½ 103rd F A Brigade's relief by 87th F A Brigade complete.	
	10	8-9am	Enemy transport heard by infantry on road at U 17 a 5 0 and fired on	
	11		Enemy TrenchMortars silenced on our front by 18-pr fire on enemy Front Line and Support Line	
	12		Registration was successfully carried out on cert in well-defined points on this Sector.	
	13	4-gun	Enemy shelled PLOEGSTEERT church with 5.9" Howitzer shells without any appreciable damage. Wire-cutting at two points was carried out (a) U 15 a 6 6 and (b) U 23 c 3 4	
	14		Wire-cutting was continued without retaliation on the enemy's part	
	15		Wire-cutting for the impending raid was completed and registration carried out by Howitzers to support attack	
	16		Results of raid carried out by 56th Infantry on this front very good One man only was slightly wounded and upwards of 20 enemy dead were left in his trenches while five prisoners were made.	

Army Form C. 2118.

WAR DIARY
or
INTELLIGENCE SUMMARY

(Erase heading not required.)

Instructions regarding War Diaries and Intelligence Summaries are contained in F. S. Regs., Part II. and the Staff Manual respectively. Title pages will be prepared in manuscript.

Place	Date	Hour	Summary of Events and Information	Remarks and references to Appendices
T 23 c 4 2	17		Extensive aggression was carried out against the enemy's front system of trenches which failed to rouse him to assume an active part in affairs.	
	18		A scheme of night firing directed against the main traffic routes the enemy is likely to use at night for his transport was carried out by the batteries of this Brigade. Routes were chosen which the batteries could easily enfilade 200 rounds per battery were expended.	
	19		Minenwerfer activity was the chief feature of this day.	
	20		C/87 cut wire at U 15 d 8 8. and no enemy fire was reported all day.	
	21		HYDE PARK CORNER was fired on by the enemy and active aggression was carried on by our batteries. German balloon was brought down by one of our aeroplanes. at 1.0 PM N. of WARNETON.	
	22		18 round s were fired at cupola at U 21 b 6½ 4 One direct hit was obtained and much wire was thrown up.	
	23		No firing took place on either side during this day.	
	24		Enemy Trench Mort r along edge of PLOEGSTEERT wood was effectively silenced by our Medium Trench Mortars. Position lately vacated by C/87 at T 17 b 0 6 was shelled with 4.2" and one pit hit and damaged Hostile aeroplane flew over STEEL TREE but apparently its presence was not divulged as no hostile fire was directed against it.	

Army Form C. 2118.

WAR DIARY
or
INTELLIGENCE SUMMARY.
(Erase heading not required)

Place	Date	Hour	Summary of Events and Information	Remarks and references to Appendices
T 23 c 4 2	25		No firing took place on either side during this day.	
	26		Two enemy aeroplanes attempted to cross our lines but after an inglorious effort hurriedly withdrew under the fire of our anti-aircraft guns. Enemy carried on active repairs of front line trench	
	27		An enemy sausage balloon having got free from BAPAUME and having crossed and re-crossed the hostile lines arrived over the area rearward of KEMMEL HILL It was engaged by our anti-aircraft guns and seven aeroplanes and brought down one mile E of DRANOUTRE in a burning condition with one prisoner under the car. Valuable documents were captured though the prisoner was exceedingly taciturn.	
	28		Retaliation was given for en my H T Ms	
	29		Germans were seen in the open. Wirecutting was carried out during the day with indifferent effect.	
	30		Wirecutting operations proceeded much more satisfactorily during the day. The enemy's parapet was also considerably damaged. Preparations for impending night raid complete. The infantry appear satisfied.	

Most Confidential

JD247

Army Form C. 2118.

VOL 1S

Instructions regarding War Diaries and Intelligence
Summaries are contained in F. S. Regs., Part II.
and the Staff Manual respectively. Title pages
will be prepared in manuscript.

WAR DIARY
87th F.A. or BRIGADE
INTELLIGENCE SUMMARY.

(Erase heading not required.)

Place	Date	Hour	Summary of Events and Information	Remarks and references to Appendices
PLOEGSTEERTE	October 1		The result of the raid was reported but owing to the escort being wounded in No man's land they had to be shot on the way across.	
	2		Brigade moved out of action to the back area, and went into rest billets around THIUSHOEK	
	5/6		The Brigade entrained at GODEWAERSVELDE travelled via CHOQUES ST POL DOULLENS to CANDAS, whence immediately on detrainment a march was made to VAUCHELLES where the Brigade went into bivouac for the night	
	7		A further march was made to bivouac immediately South of COUIN Meantime reconnaissance was carried out by Brigade and Battery Commanders with a view to occupation of positions South of HEBUTERNE	
	8		Work was carried on preparing positions S. of HEBUTERNE	
	11/12		18-pr batteries moved into action to occupy their wire-cutting positions and dumping of ammunition was begun. At the same time the Brigade came under and "Artillery Group" and assumed responsibility for the defence of the line	
	13		Night firing was carried out on a track and railway frequented by the enemy	
	13/16		Wire-cutting was begun and continued throughout this and the three succeeding days. The front line wire was effectively dealt with by a combination of Trench Mortar and 18-pr fire and registration on all wire up to and including the third line was finally completed.	

Army Form C. 2118.

WAR DIARY
114 F.A. or BRIGADE INTELLIGENCE SUMMARY

(Erase heading not required.)

Instructions regarding War Diaries and Intelligence Summaries are contained in F. S. Regs., Part II and the Staff Manual respectively. Title pages will be prepared in manuscript.

Place	Date	Hour	Summary of Events and Information	Remarks and references to Appendices
CONSTANCE TRENCH	Oct 16		The Brigade received notice that relief would take place at 6.0 PM the same evening. Batteries pulled out and withdrew to their wagon lines	
	17		Brigade marched to new wagon lines on the western side of the ALBERT- Aveley road, thence proceeded straight into action west of THIEPVAL. Great difficulty was experienced in getting the guns into action. Rain fell all the night of the 17th/18th and dawn saw vehicles bogged in the mud. A/87 got their guns into action before dawn with one exception. With the morning the rain slackened and the initial difficulties were overcome.	
	18		Registration was successfully carried out in spite of adverse weather conditions. Salient points were checked by the Brigade Commanders	
	19		Message was received that the attack on REGINA TRENCH timed for Thursday 19th October was postponed for two days. Wirecutting and accurate registration was continued as far as was possible under the adverse conditions which prevailed. The proposed day of the attack was exceptionally wet but the succeeding two days afforded a strong contrast to their immediate predecessors. The 21st was free from rain though bright sunshine did not prevail	
	21		At 12.6 PM the infantry crossed the front line and within 20 minutes the prisoners began to appear over the STUFF REDOUBT crest. This had the effect of many successes on the men manning the guns. The prisoners were Bavarians and seemed either of rather youthful or mature age	

Army Form C. 2118.

WAR DIARY
9th F.A. or BRIGADE
INTELLIGENCE SUMMARY.

(Erase heading not required.)

Instructions regarding War Diaries and Intelligence Summaries are contained in F. S. Regs., Part II. and the Staff Manual respectively. Title pages will be prepared in manuscript.

Place	Date	Hour	Summary of Events and Information	Remarks and references to Appendices
CONSTANCE TRENCH	OCTOBER 21		The barrages in the following form :- From Zero to plus 1½ minutes the 18-prs. were divided so as to form (1) a creeping barrage (2) a standing barrage on REGINA TRENCH (the objective) and (3) a rabbit sheet-searching and sweeping to a distance 200 yards N. of the objective. The 4.5" Howitzer formed a longitudinal barrage on the left flank Onlookers from direct enfilade were astonished at the accuracy with which the Artillery Barrage advanced in front of the infantry In the succeeding phases the barrage conformed to the infantry's advance	
	22-4		These three days were occupied in active preparations for the GRAND-COUR RT battle. The Brigade zone was chosen as a longitudinal belt running up towards the S.W. corner of GRANDCOURT Night firing was also carried out intermittently on the new enemy defences, and especially on a new trench about 300 yards to the N. of the captured REGINA TRENCH. Wirecutting was begun on any wire visible in the Brigade Zone. There was, however little or no wire visible.	
	25		Notification was receive that postponement till the 29th had been resolved. Thus the daily aggressive programme was carried on	
	27-30		A further postponement was announced. Extremely adverse weather conditions characterised the 28th, 29th, and 30th	
	31		Information was received at about midnight that a probable date for the operation was fixed for the 5th prox. The 31st was a contrast from the weather point of view to its immediate predecessors. Meantime a more aggressive programme was issued to the batteries	
	26		OMISSA :- On the At 5.0 AM the enemy opened a heavy barrage on our front and at 5.25 AM in response to the S.O.S. rocket signal the Brigade opened a barrage on their S.O.S. lines. The attack was easily repulsed and 41 prisoners were taken	

WAR DIARY
or
INTELLIGENCE SUMMARY.
(Erase heading not required.)

Army Form C. 2118.

8?th R.F.?

Vol 16

Place	Date	Hour	Summary of Events and Information	Remarks and references to Appendices
CONSTANCE TRENCH	NOVEMBER 3		Exceptional aerial activity was a marked feature of this day. One enemy plane in particular returned successively over our lines between MOUQUET FARM and THIEPVAL. At 4 pm the enemy bombarded our battery positions in R 32 b.	
		7	An intense bombardment was opened by the V Corps on our left at 12.50 pm lasting about 15 minutes. The enemy shelled LUCKY WAY at its junction with STUFF TRENCH practically flattening the former.	
		8	Brigad. O.P. was commenced in SPLUTTER TRENCH Our action consisted in intermittent shelling of the ANCRE bridges during the day.	
		9	Again marked aerial activity on the enemy's part resulting in one of our fighting machines being forced to descend. The enemy counter-battery work was actively carried out on our position in R.32.b & 0 with 5.9" How.	
		10	The enemy bombarded our battery positions in R 32 b and 33a with gas shells all through the night beginning at 11 pm and continuing up till the hour of commencement of our intense bombardment at 6.30 am. This intense bombardment was effectively carried out according to programme. A feeble reply was put up to this except on SCHWABEN which was heavily bombarded.	
		11	The enemy shelled R 33 a at 1.am. Enemy night aerial activity began to be marked. Bomb-dropping expeditions were carried out in the moonlight on ALBERT and the rearward area generally. An aeroplane was observed to fall in flames (identity unknown) about 10.40 pm. STUFF REDOUBT was also intermittently shelled	

Army Form C. 2118.

WAR DIARY
or
INTELLIGENCE SUMMARY.
(Erase heading not required.)

Place	Date	Hour	Summary of Events and Information	Remarks and references to Appendices
	NOVEMBER /2.		The enemy's defences were kept under a continuous Shrapnel and H.E. fire during the day. MOUQUET FARM and SPLUTTER TRENCH were the localities most actively engaged. A marked feature was the entire absence of our own and enemy aircraft. Ground in "No Man's Land" reported very heavy.	
	/3.		The Brigad F.O.O. reported that at 5.45 am the barrage opened simultaneously over the whole area. The infantry thought it very good and advanced right home up under it. They met with no opposition and found the enemy quite unprepared, having grown accustomed to ou barrage in the early morning. Thus the infantry reached their objective with ease. The enemy counter-barrage was slow in being put up and feeble in its event. The capture of HANSA LINE, and with it ST. PIERRE DIVION, also BEAUMONT HAMEL was announced by the Corps on our left, at about 11 am.	
	/4		The enemy seemed to be under the impression that we held a more advanced line tgan we really did, for he opened a heavy barrage on a trench in advance of our front line, flattening it out. The raid carried out by the infantry had a measure of success.	
	/5		The enemy was active with his aeroplanes during the day and also during the night, he again dropped bombs on the rearward area	
	/6		Opportunity targets were engaged - mostly parties of infantry observed N. of the ANCRE. Considerable movement of the enemy was seen during the day.	
	/7		The ANCRE bridges were desultorily shelled during the day. The infantry were reported to be consolidating a winter line The enemy opened a heavy fire with guns of various calibre N. of the ANCRE whereupon till the situation cleared we opened a slow rate of fire on our S.O.S. lines The situation was reported clear.	

Army Form C. 2118.

WAR DIARY
or
INTELLIGENCE SUMMARY.
(Erase heading not required.)

Instructions regarding War Diaries and Intelligence Summaries are contained in F. S. Regs., Part II. and the Staff Manual respectively. Title pages will be prepared in manuscript.

Place	Date	Hour	Summary of Events and Information	Remarks and references to Appendices
X.16.c.9.	NOVEMBER 22.		Mist hung over the landscape and observation was impossible till 1 pm when fresh positions were reconnoitred around THIEPVAL with a view to more effectively severing the new front N. of the ANCRE taken over on this day. Positions suitable for clearing the crest and at the same time out of view of the dominating SERRE RIDGE were unobtainable so it was resolved to remain in the present positions. SCHWABEN REDOUBT and HANSA LINE was bombarded by the enemy during the afternoon.	
	23.		The enemy were observed dropping short into GRANDCOURT. He shelled BEAUCOURT - SUR - ANCRE during the afternoon	
	23.		Our probable relief on the 4th prox. was announced, and we commenced vigorously to collect the stacks of empty cases which lay all around the area. This work was continued up till the last day of the month.	
	29.		18-pr fire was carried out this morning at 1 am on PUISIEUX TRENCH lasting ¾ of an hour. At 6 pm a response was given to an infantry call for retaliation. This fire was continued till the hostile shelling had ceased. A combined bombardment with Gas shell and	
	30		By order of 19th D.A. Fire was opened on S.O.S lines at 5.35 am "All Quiet" was reported by our Liaison Officer and after maintaining fire for 20 minutes we stopped.	

2353 Wt: W2544/1454 700,000 5/15 D. D. & L. A.D.S.S./Forms/C. 2118.

WAR DIARY
or
INTELLIGENCE SUMMARY.

(Erase heading not required.)

87 B.U.R. Army Dec 17

Place	Date	Hour	Summary of Events and Information	Remarks and references to Appendices
			December.1916.	
			1st) WE continued to salvage material,and made large stacks	
			2nd)-of empty cartridge cases which were handed over to the	
			3rd) charge of the D.A.C. The ammunition was collected and	
			placed in boxes which were stacked in dug-outs & gun-pits	
			4th. We moved out of action,everything working very smoothly.	
			5th. Remained at wagon-lines.Billeting parties were sent out	
			in advance.	
			6th. We marched out of the wagon-lines near ALBERT.and arrived	
			that afternoon at AMPLIER.	
			8th. Left AMPLIER and marched to GEZAINCOURT.	
			16th. Left GEZAINCOURT and marched to SARTON.where we remained	
			to the end of the month.	
			25th. All the Batteries had preparedsplendid dinners for the	
			men on this day and the C.O. went round all the Batteries	
			whilst the men were having their dinners.	

Lieut-Colonel R.F.A

Commanding 87th.F.A.Brigade.

87 Bde R.A Vol 18
Army Form C. 2118.

WAR DIARY
or
INTELLIGENCE SUMMARY.
(Erase heading not required.)

Instructions regarding War Diaries and Intelligence Summaries are contained in F.S. Regs., Part II. and the Staff Manual respectively. Title pages will be prepared in manuscript.

Place	Date	Hour	Summary of Events and Information	Remarks and references to Appendices
	JANUARY 1917			
SARTON	2nd		The Brigade moved from SARTON. H.Q. and D/87 being stationed in THIÈVRES. The other Batteries moved into action in front of COLINCAMP, being attached in the following manner A/87 - K.32.a.8.4 attached to 42nd Brigade	
COLINCAMP			B/87 - K.27.c.1.9 " " 40" "	
			C/87 - K.27.a.5.8 " " 28" "	
SAILLY-AU-BOIS	15th		The Brigade moved into action in front SAILLY-AU-BOIS and occupied positions allotted to them. 19" Divisional Artillery was formed into two groups. Right being Commanded by Lieut-Col W.T.KENT. R.F.A. and the Left by Colonel TOVEY 9/87 being attached to the Left. Attached to Right Group were B/86 and three Batteries of 155" Brigade R.F.A. Observation being difficult; little firing being done, Registration carried out when possible. Weather being cold. Heavy fall of snow and frost found.	
	18th		Observation still difficult; hindering work of registration, Enemy Artillery active, shelling intermittently in the vicinity of our Batteries. No damage done	
	19th to 21st		Enemy aeroplanes active, Enemy second and third lines kept under fire during the night. Registration continued. Group night firing Programme carried out: 6 small Balloons seen at K.27.6. Hostile aeroplane flew over K.20 - K.21 - K.26 - and K.27.	
	22nd to 25th		Enemy's Communication Trenches, Trench Junctions, Roads, Tracks, Etc. Kept under fire. Night firing carried out as usual. Hostile fire Normal. A few prison shells fell in the vicinity of Battery Position.	
	26th		Night firing carried out as usual, fronts engaged:- La LOUVIÈRE FARM. LIGHT RAILWAY, Trench Junctions, STAR ALLEY and all Enemy out/post lines. Counter Battery work carried out at L.14. C.3.2½. Retaliation given at request of Infantry. Enemy aeroplanes active, flying high.	
	27th		Group firing Carried out by Divisional orders, on Enemy first, second and third lines, Targets engaged in co operation with R.F.C.	
	28th		Observation bad, Infantry reported flashes of 2 guns at L.20.c.2.3. Hostile fire quiet, night firing as usual, burst of fire on Enemy lines.	
	29th		Night firing as usual. A Group Bombardment carried out at various times of the day. Observation bad.	
	31st			

31/1/17.

Alan T. Butler
Lieut-Colonel R.F.A.
Commanding 87th F.A. Brigade.

WAR DIARY or INTELLIGENCE SUMMARY

(Erase heading not required.)

Army Form C. 2118.

87 Bde RFA VM19

Place	Date	Hour	Summary of Events and Information	Remarks and references to Appendices
	FEBRUARY 1st To		C/87th still attached to LEFT GROUP. 87th Bde continues to form RIGHT GROUP with B/86 & A.B. & D/155 attached. Work on Battery Positions and offensive positions making steady progress. Registration of enemy front difficult, owing to thick mist. A Group Bombardment was carried out at midnight 2nd/3rd on the 1st, 2nd and 3rd lines and communication trenches of the enemy. On the 3rd A.B. & D/155 were	
	3rd		detached from the Brigade, which now forms CENTRE GROUP with B/86th attached.	
	4th To 6th		Registration carried on, when possible but observation was practically impossible owing to thick mists. Enemy on the 4th instant shelled Battery Positions and obtained a direct hit on No 1 gun 7/87, there were no casualties, but the gun was considerably damaged, sight and carriage being knocked to pieces. Special attention was paid by all Batteries to the enemy's wire.	
	7th 9th		Hostile aeroplanes very active, one flew very low over Battery Positions apparently with the intention of taking photographs. A Bombardment on the enemy wire carried out 9th day, apparently with good results. Hostile aeroplanes active, one flying low seemed to be observing for its enemy shelled all round Battery Position. During the night, S.O.S. was called for Regimental Support was given by all Batteries.	
	10th		Rehearsal of barrage support of an Infantry raid carried out. Hostile aeroplanes active. At 8.30 p.m. we had 5 minute intense barrage on enemy front and support lines.	
	11th 12th 13th		Canadian Division on our right during their attack on TEN TREE ALLEY, by keeping a barrage on enemy front and support division. We supported a raid by the Infantry, by a heavy barrage on support lines and back area. Enemy relief suspected to-day. Brigade kept all tracks, roads, trench junction and communication trenches under shell of fire.	
	16th		1 Hour Bombardment carried out at 3 p.m. on enemy's lines and back area. Enemies between our own and enemy aeroplane. Hostile plane brought down, our plane forced to descend in vicinity of Battery Position, owing to pilot being wounded	
	17th 18th		Batteries R.B./166 are once more attached to this Brigade Battery B/86 detached from this Brigade	

Army Form C. 2118.

WAR DIARY
or
INTELLIGENCE SUMMARY.
(Erase heading not required.)

Place	Date	Hour	Summary of Events and Information	Remarks and references to Appendices
	19th		Took guns out of pits, so as to enable us to get a greater switch on Right and Left. This to support LEFT GROUP enemy offensive action, obtained line hits on nos 1 & 3 gun pits of A/156.	
	20th to 23rd		Fight very hard. Registration impossible. Used night firing carried out. Enemy shelled HEBUTERNE and the plain daily. A few gas shells were sent over. On the 21st C/87 were shelled, enemy obtaining a direct hit on the Cook House; Two men being killed and another man gassed. The latter sent to Field Ambulance.	
	23rd		Some taken out of their pits into the open, so as to enable us to cover the Left Group Front.	
	24th		Fight still hard. Day quiet. D/87, at night, shelled PUISIEUX with gas shells, in conjunction with Corps Heavy Artillery. News came through, to day, that the enemy was retiring, and that we had occupied SERRE. Order given to all Batteries to cease all fire until further information was forthcoming.	
	25th		A & B/155 were detached from this Brigade. C/87 was now under the orders of this Brigade, and moved into a more advanced position K.27.d.2.2. on the Plain.	
	26th		Teams were got up for A, B, & D Batteries to move into more advanced positions. This order, however, was cancelled and they remained in their old positions.	
	27th		Today we reconnoitred to find advanced positions for the Brigade. These were selected just behind our old front line, and Batteries were ordered to advance at night. A large party was sent out to make a track for the guns. Orders were again cancelled, and all Batteries returned to their old positions, except D/87 who occupied a new advanced position at K.15.d.1.2.	

Oliver R. Pilk[?] [signature]
Lieut-Colonel R.F.A
Commanding 87th F.A Brigade

WAR DIARY or INTELLIGENCE SUMMARY

Army Form C. 2118

87th BRIGADE R.F.A.

N°20

Place	Date	Hour	Summary of Events and Information	Remarks and references to Appendices
	MARCH			
	1st to 4th		Huns still continue good & enemy still retreating. 87 Bde advanced Light Section into No Mans Land at K24 a.±.8. Remaining 4 guns & also 9/87 moved to more advanced positions in K24 a.±.8. so as to be able to cover our zone. T.M. personnel have been attached to us for the purpose of making roads to the advance of batteries. There are also supplying parties to assist in the work.	
	5th		8/77 & 9/87 advanced over new road & trolley way to positions near STAR WOOD for the purpose of wire cutting in front of BUCQUOY.	
	6th/7th		8/87 & 9/87 registered guns in new positions. 9/87 (forward section) & 9/87 kept up bursts of fire intermittently on two roads at F.27.b.50.50 – F.26 d.70.10.	
	8th		9/87 & 8/87 wire cutting. They also took part in bombardments to support Infantry advance on BUCQUOY	
	9th		9/87 (forward section) 8/87 & 9/87 were relieved by 11th Division. H.Q. personnel moved to Bayen Lines	
	10th		Batteries A/87 C/87 received guns from 11th & 11/79w . H.Q. Personnel moved to Bayen Lines	
	11th		Brigade marched to OUTRESSONS via LOIGNEUX, THIEVRES, SARTON & DOULLENS. The Brigade was inspected by the C.R.A.	
	12th		Brigade marched to HUBROMETZ.	
	13th		Brigade marched to HEUCHIN via INVIN.	
	14th		Brigade resting & cleaning up. Batteries were inspected by C.O.	
	15th		Brigade marched to MAZINGHEM via FE RIN PALFART- RELY-ROMBLY	
	16th		Resting & general cleaning up.	
	17th		Brigade marched to MORBECQUE via AIRE & STEENBECQUE.	
	18th		Brigade marched to NEUF BERQUIN thence to MERVILLE	
	19th/20th		Resting & cleaning up.	
	21st		Brigade marched to DRANOUTRE via OUTERSTEENE & BAILLEUL. The Brigade is attached to 36th Division for billets & rations.	
	22nd		Brigade H.Q. moved to HUGHES FARM near BAILLEUL.	
	23rd/26th		Batteries undergoing thorough inspection & training when possible.	
	27th		C/87 sent a working party to K136 (advanced position) to camouflage the position. All Batteries training & cleaning up. Echelons were filled	
	29th		Orders received to go into action on 2nd April. Battery Commanders went out today to reconnoitre their positions	
	30th/31st		9/87 again working on advanced position. All Batteries training	

3/3/17

Olrun F H Knut
A/Lt Lt-Col R.F.A
Comg 87th F.A. Brigade

87 Bde RFA
Vol 21

Army Form C. 2118.

WAR DIARY or INTELLIGENCE SUMMARY.
(Erase heading not required.)

Place	Date	Hour	Summary of Events and Information	Remarks and references to Appendices
	April 1st		Batteries standing by.	
	2nd/3rd		On the night of the 2nd/3rd the Batteries moved into action under the SPANBROEK GROUP	
	5th/6th		On the night of the 5th/6th the Batteries came out of action.	
	6th		Brigade marched to CAMPAGNE via DRANOUTRE, BAILLEUL, STRAZEELE, BORRE, HAZEBROUCK & EBBLINGHEM	
	7th		The March was continued to POLINCOVE via ARQUES, STOMER & NORDAUSQUES	
	8th		Cleaning up.	
	9th-11th		Training – section gun drill, signalling, laying & fuze setting, harness cleaning, shooting drill, young officers' hands. Lectures to officers	
	12th-13th		75 on 92-112 with addition of Battery Staff training	
	14th		Inspection by R.O.C. RFA	
	15th		Cleaning up. Brigade sports unfortunately curtailed owing to bad weather.	
	16th		Inspection by G.O.C. 19th Div.: afternoon parade.	
	17th		Gun drill, harness cleaning etc	
	18th		Officers' Gymkhana – very successful – General 19th Div present.	
	19th		Inspection by C.O. of Batteries for Bty in full marching order/packing up	
	20th		Brigade marched to CAMPAGNE via STOMER & ARQUES	
	21st		To EECKE via ABBLINGHEM, HAZEBROUCK & CAESTRE	
	22nd		To wagon lines near METEUTRE via GODEWAERSVELDE & BOESCHEPE	
	23rd		H.Q. do not go into action	
	24th		Batteries go into action under Col Tovey – DIEPENDAHL GROUP.	
	25th		Registration	
	26th		Drawing of material & working on MAGNUM OPUS position	
	29th		Orders to withdraw from action r/take over from 102nd Bde 23rd Bn. same night. One section per Bty move up by night	
	30th		Relief complete on night of 30th April/1st May. HQ + Btys Wagon lines + forward positions established.	

B Jones
Lt Major RFA
Cmdg 87th F.A. Brigade

87 Bde RFA
Vol 2.2

Army Form C. 2118.

WAR DIARY
or
INTELLIGENCE SUMMARY.
(Erase heading not required.)

Instructions regarding War Diaries and Intelligence Summaries are contained in F.S. Regs., Part II. and the Staff Manual respectively. Title pages will be prepared in manuscript.

Place	Date	Hour	Summary of Events and Information	Remarks and references to Appendices
YPRES	1/5/17		Direct hit on B/87; C/87 shelled.	
	2/5/17		300 or 400 rounds were fired on A/87. There being 3 slight casualties	
	3/5/17/6		During this period, YPRES & the battery positions were subjected to heavy shelling most of two daily. Work on our own Magnum Opus	
	10/5/17		position proceeded regularly. A. B. & May D/87 obtained 2 OK's & several Y's being in cooperation with one of our planes. On the following day. They again had successfully with aeroplane registration	
	9/5/17		C/87 were shelled out. 2/Lt J.B. Barnes being killed.	
	9/10R		On this night the enemy rushed our front line trenches in spite of our precautionary shelling	
	10/11R			
	11/4		Under cover of our own [section for B/87 moved from YPRES to the wagon lines near WESTOUTRE	
			From 7-11am D/87 were heavily shelled a were B/87 from 11.30am - 2 pm. 1 gun in the last case being completely destroyed. Later in the afternoon C/87 had 2 guns put out of action. In the course of heavy shelling	
KLEINE VIERSTRAAT FARM	11/12R		H.Q. & the remaining sections of the batteries moved to the wagon lines, 1 section of the battery going into action around KLEINE VIERSTRAAT	*(N.10.a.b.5)
	12/13R		H.Q. & remaining sections moved into action Lt-Col (Ent: Cmdg) DIEPENDAAL GROUP with his HQ at LA CLYTTE. (FROM	
	13R		Aeroplane shots	
	14R			
	15R		Enemy aeroplane active	
	16R		Wire cutting commenced along front guest day	
			Shoot registration on our	
			B/87 changed position on the third to KLEINE VIERSTRAAT FARM	
	14-16R		On this night an exploited an enemy dump on OBSTEL TRENCH. There was no result. The trench being empty.	
	16/17R		HQ moved to advanced position alongside B/87 at KLEINE VIERSTRAAT FARM. The Brigade being now part of the DIEPENDAAL GROUP.	
	18R		Commanded by Lt-Col T.H. Rochdale D.S.O. Hostile aeroplane active	
	18/19R		The Brigade received a raid by the 7th Bde on 7th NAP'S NOSE	
	19R		Between 4 & 5 pm. D/87 put up a covering fire on OBR SUPPORT for the trench Mortars	
	20R		Vigorous wire cutting was carried on	(PTO)

Army Form C. 2118.

WAR DIARY
or
INTELLIGENCE SUMMARY.
(Erase heading not required.)

Instructions regarding War Diaries and Intelligence Summaries are contained in F.S. Regs., Part II. and the Staff Manual respectively. Title pages will be prepared in manuscript.

Place	Date	Hour	Summary of Events and Information	Remarks and references to Appendices
	May 21st		The Kite Balloon Section now became available for registering batteries on invisible targets.	
	22nd		D/87 again put up a covering fire in OBIT SUPPORT for the Trench Mortars	
	23rd		B/88 attacked to the Brigade, one section moving into action by night (23/24th)	
	24/25R		B/88's now complete	
	25R		3/bn MORSANO	
			C/87 was shelled out 1 officer & 2 O.R. makes being wounded & an ammunition dump with 550 rounds being blown up. From	
		3pm–4.30pm	D/87 carried OBLIGE SUPPORT & RESERVE repeating this from 6pm–7pm	
	25/26R		In the night the Right Battalion supported by barrage of A.B. & C/87, raided the enemy lines in an effort to secure identification of enemy units. C/87 were shelled out	
	26R		The Groups under the 192 B.A. were reformed into the Right Group (Lt-Col Halsall cmdg) & Left Group (Major Nelson cmdg). A.B. & D/87 together with 9/177 became responsible for the defence of the line from O.7.c.4.5. to the SOUCHEZ ROAD (Right Group Front). Lt-Col W.J KENT commanding Meantime C/87 came under the orders of the Left Group Commander.	
	26/27th 28/29th		In the afternoon a violent artillery duel developed many dumps were blown up. A.B. & C/87 handed over to A/156, C/155 & A/252 respectively. Themselves moving into Funlloquin Caves poitus. During the night HQ/87 position came under heavy fire.	
	29/30R		There was a redistribution of batteries in the 192 B.A. The whole of the Brigade together took B. & C/177 was formed into "B" Sub Group of the Right Group, Lt-Col KENT being the Sub Group Commander & Lt-Col RICHOLME in command of the Group. H.Q. again shelled	
	13-31st		During the period work on M.O. posters was carried on, & were cutting proceeded vigorously	

Maurice Field
Lt Col 879
for Lt-Col 870
Cmdg 87 F.A. Brigade

WAR DIARY
or
INTELLIGENCE SUMMARY

87 Bde R.F.A Vol 23

Place: LOCRE HERSOM SECT

Date	Hour	Summary of Events and Information	Remarks
1st June 2nd June 3rd 5th		From 6 to 6.10 pm a Boche barrage was carried out. H.Q. C/87 & D/87 were heavily shelled. Heavy artillery fighting throughout the day.	
7th		H.Q. position was lightly shelled in the morning, a few shells bursting in the actual yard. Batteries hit up at intervals. In the afternoon the C.O. Brig'de co-operated with the powerful artillery action of another Divn & 20 prisoners were taken during the morning. B/87 & D/87 Batteries moved to a forward position. The wagon lines re coming further forward.	
10th 12th 13th 15th 19th 20th 21/22nd 23rd 24th 25th 27th 28th 29th 30th		The Batteries again moved forward. H/Q. moved to B position to next original 2nd line trench The Wagon Lines moved to positions wrest of SIEGE FARM. Advanced section moved forward. The Brigade relieved in the line by the 177th F.A.Bde. retired to the wagon line The Brigade marched to rest in the BOIS de BERINGHEN area via CLYTE-la-CLYTE-LOCRE H.Q. at MONT ROUGE Cleaning up & training. Tactical Schemes carried out by officers MCO's Reconnaissance & forward observation. C.O. inspected B/87 in various wagon lines. G.O.C. 19th Divn inspected R. Brigade in Field Service Marching Order One section per Bty relieved battery section of 177th Bde in action Relief of 177th F.A.Brigade completed H.Q. at N.17.d.3.4. Wagon lines changed position. D/87 heavily shelled.	

30/6/17

W.L. Kerd
Lieut Col 87
Comdg 87 F.A Brigade

87 FA Bde
Nº 2

WAR DIARY
or
INTELLIGENCE SUMMARY.
(Erase heading not required.)

Army Form C. 2118.

Place	Date	Hour	Summary of Events and Information	Remarks and references to Appendices
HQ 87 FA Bde at N.17.c.3.4	July			
	1st-8th		During this period, hostile artillery were comparatively inactive. On the 6th Aeroplanes on the 8th Hun planes were very active, one of our observing planes being brought down on the former date.	
	9/10th		On the night of the 9/10th operations carried out in conjunction with the infantry resulted in the capture of prisoners & the enemy ground in the vicinity of TOOL FARM	
	11th		2 Boche aeroplanes came over this afternoon & brought down 3 of our balloons	
	12th		Todays hostile machine was brought down near WERVICQ. In later part of the evening A/87 were shelled	
	13th		Air fights were very common today. About 11pm the front line was barraged & retaliation given.	
	14th		Our front line was again heavily barraged at 8.45 – 9.10pm, 1 command of Lt. A/87 were shelled	
	15th		C/315 & D/315 were attached to this Brigade, the whole forming the Right Group. Lt. Col. Kent commanding.	
	16th		Retaliation was twice given at the request of the Infantry.	
	17th		M/6 were now attached to the Group	
	18th		In the evening we put up a barrage for an infantry operation. Prisoners resulting despite the enemy's retaliatory barrage. The enemy again barraged on our attack about 5am	
	19/7/17			
	20th		In the course of the day D/315 fired with hidden howitzers.	
	21st		Both hostile artillery & aircraft were exceptionally active in conjunction with R.H.T.M.B's. A/87 bombarded	
			BOMB FORM etc	

(PTO)

Army Form C. 2118.

WAR DIARY
or
INTELLIGENCE SUMMARY.
(Erase heading not required.)

Instructions regarding War Diaries and Intelligence Summaries are contained in F. S. Regs., Part II. and the Staff Manual respectively. Title pages will be prepared in manuscript.

Place	Date	Hour	Summary of Events and Information	Remarks and references to Appendices
	July			
	22nd		The enemy aircraft were extremely active	
	22nd/23rd		Subsequent to a practice Barrage further Buildings were taken & lost again. 6 Enemies being taken in the course of the fighting. The enemy merely put up a light barrage in retaliation for our.	
	24th		Flying very low, hostile planes were very active in the early morning. During the afternoon 26 Zeppgood targets together with 51st HA Group	
	24/25		Hostile artillery fired heavily with gas etc on the front area during the night. Our planes were again active	
	25		Quiet, save that 76th in conjunction with 7 R.H.T.M's bombarded further Buildings & Broodseinde Cabaret at night 7 enemy fire of gun shells in ONSAET & OOSTTAVERNE woods.	
	28th		Hostile Planes lively.	
	29th		0.315 Spasmodically Hostile retaliated to heavy enemy shelling	
	22nd–30th		During the period wire cutting was carried out daily & night firing was directed against specially selected points, tracks etc, also with a view to keeping open all gaps made in the enemy wire. Meantime the Divisional Artillery Groups had been reorganised for the attack, all the batteries of the Brigade being for a period to the command of Lt Col W.S Tovey comdg Left Arty Group, while Headquarters of the Bde were alternately acting as HQ of the Right Arty Group (Lt Col W. Kent comdg), comprising the 23rd, 124th Brigades together with 146, C/46, D/46, A/315 & B/315.	

Army Form C. 2118.

WAR DIARY
or
INTELLIGENCE SUMMARY.
(Erase heading not required.)

Place	Date	Hour	Summary of Events and Information	Remarks and references to Appendices
	July			
	31st		Ultimately, at 3.50 a.m. the 31st infantry & artillery co-operated in the unsuccessful attack launched. The original Reg'tl Group (ie 87d Bde Batteries plus 2B/5, D/3/5 + A/46), now reformed support the infantry in the work of consolidation.	

W.D. Kerr
Lieut-Col R.F.A.
Cmdg. 87th A Brigade

WAR DIARY or INTELLIGENCE SUMMARY

Army Form C. 2118.

87 Bde S.A.A
Vol 25

Place	Date	Hour	Summary of Events and Information	Remarks and references to Appendices
N.17.c.3.d NEWPORT (NR BAILLEUL)	August 1st 1917		Subsequent to the successful attack on 31st July, a bill of inclement weather hampered further operations considerably. In the early days of August the activity on our front was slight. The enemy fire being mainly retaliatory. Little Casualties were apparent in the air, generally, our programme of days aright mainly were merely normal	
	5th 7th		During the night 7/8 14/87 were relieved with intermittent bursts of fire 9/46 a Retour from nolce + from the Left Group Command N.17 was 0/47. 0/315	
	8th 10th		were accorded wagons with ammunition to B4. + 8/87. Today, 8/88 + CMT each got positions. Today, Brigade Headquarters withdrew to the Wagon lines, the command of the Right group to passes to Lt Col Matock. Enemy 12/14 7A Bde A.6.1. B Batteries of the 87th Bde remained until the 20th inst. C + B/315 now withdrew from action to the Wagon lines. C/87 remained with the Left Group, Lt Col Belham Cmdg During the night 19/11 hostile aeroplanes were busy in the vicinity of the 87th Bde wagon lines	
X.17.b.6.6 (NR BAILLEUL)	11th N.19th 21st		Bde H.Q. now moved into St Jans Cappel to wagon lines in the vicinity of Bailleul Bde H.Q. at rest. Enemy Aeroplanes busy nightly dropping bombs in neighbourhood The Batteries withdrew from action to their wagon lines, ultimately their Bivouacs with a easy reach of H.Q. wagon lines	
STRAZEELE	24th 27th		The Brigade in N. Sector D.A.G. marched to the lines near Bailleul to the STRAZEELE area. The first two days were spent in cleaning up + Training programme was entered upon by the Brigade Parades including note-prime, lecture, Drill for Junior and N.C.O's + Gas Helmet Parades for N.C.O's gunners drivers + Signallers.	
	28th		The C.R.A. inspected the personnel of the Brigade to discussed with orders a assembly inspection of the Batteries + Headquarters of Brigade	

Army Form C. 2118.

WAR DIARY
or
INTELLIGENCE SUMMARY
(Erase heading not required.)

Instructions regarding War Diaries and Intelligence Summaries are contained in F.S. Regs., Part II. and the Staff Manual respectively. Title Pages will be prepared in manuscript.

Place	Date	Hour	Summary of Events and Information	Remarks and references to Appendices
STRAZEELE	29th 30th 31st	—	Brigade Commander inspected Batteries at wagon lines in Marching Parade Mounted Drill order. Setting up drill, gun drill, laying, signalling, harness cleaning, dismounting drill.	
	1/9/17			

W. Kerr
Lieut. Col. RFA
Cmdg 87th A Bde.

249 Wt. W14957/Mgo 750,000 1/16 J.B.C. & A. Forms/C.2118/12.

Army Form C. 2118.

WAR DIARY
or
INTELLIGENCE SUMMARY
(Erase heading not required.)

Instructions regarding War Diaries and Intelligence Summaries are contained in F. S. Regs., Part II. and the Staff Manual respectively. Title Pages will be prepared in manuscript.

JH 26

Place	Date	Hour	Summary of Events and Information	Remarks and references to Appendices
STRAZEELE			**87th F.A.BRIGADE - September 1917.**	
	1st		G.O.C.R.A., inspected Headquarters and Batteries in full Marching Order,Parade Mounted.	
	2nd-3rd		Training continued:Gun Drill,Laying,Fuze Setting,Signalling etc.	
	4?		G.O.C. 19th Divn. inspected 19th Divl.Artillery in Marching Order,this Brigade taking part.	
	5?			
	6?		I Section of A/87 moved up into action.	
Oyshot 28 NW 1/20000			Headquarters of this Brigade moved to Victoria Mine-Shaft (O 2 a 8 0) to take command of CANAL GROUP ARTILLERY comprising of A,B, and D/88 and A/87.The route followed in moving into action was - outskirts Bailleul - St JANS CAPPEL - MONT-ROUGE - LA CLYTTE - VIERSTRAAT.	
	7?		Enemy quiet in morning, but their Artillery active during the afternoon. Our own Artillery were especially active on YPEN-BRIELEN.	
	8?		Quiet.	
	9?&10?		Night and Day Firing Programmes carried out under orders of Group Commander.	
	9?		B/88 assisted the Heavy Artillery in a successful shoot.	
	10?		Hostile Aircraft very active.	
	11?		On the night 10/11th the Group supported a raid by the Infantry, for the purpose of identification.	
	11?		The CANAL GROUP became known as "A" Sub-Group, Commanded by Lt-Col W.J.Kent R.F.A., as heretofore.	
	12?		The Group now comprising A,B and D/88 and A and D/18, and working under the Right Group 19th D.A., Commanded by Lt-Col G.S.TOVEY D.S.O.,carried out a bombardment of Tracks, Roads and Dug-outs by way of Night Firing.	
	15?		Commencing at 8 a.m. on the 15th the Sub-Group joined in CORPS BARRAGE No.I.In the afternoon the position of D/88 was shelled with 10.5 c.m;s. During the day the enemy artillery was active, and his aircraft displayed abnormal liveliness.Bombs were dropped in the vicinity of VERMOOZEELE, and 4 balloons were seen to be observing.	
	16?		C/236 now joined the Sub-Group. Night Firing was carried out as from the night of 15/16th on the "TASK" principle i.e. specially selected points were subjected to bombardment.	

WAR DIARY
or
INTELLIGENCE SUMMARY
(Erase heading not required.)

Army Form C. 2118.

Place	Date	Hour	Summary of Events and Information	Remarks and references to Appendices
	16th		At 10 a.m. the Sub-Group joined in ARMY BARRAGE No.1, to which the enemy replied to heavily, hostile machines also being active. For the rest, Tracks and Roads were the objects of our Day Firing.	
	16th-19th 17th 18th		Night and Day Firing were carried out as usual. The Sub-Group assisted in CORPS BARRAGE No.4 at 5 p.m.	
	19th 20th		All batteries under our command joined in ARMY BARRAGE No.2 at 6 a.m., CORPS BARRAGE No.5 at 12 noon and again in ARMY BARRAGE No.3 at 8.30 p.m. The enemy Artillery were more or less active throughout the day. The final CORPS BARRAGE (No.7) was fired beginning at 3 p.m.	
	22nd		This was "ATTACK DAY". At 5.40 a.m. the assault was launched, the Infantry moving forward under a powerful Barrage. Headquarters of this Brigade now took over command of the LEFT GROUP with Lt.Col W.J.KENT Commanding. Comprising this Group were Sub-Groups 3 and 4, the first under the command of Lt.Col A.C.GORDON D.S.O., and the second under the orders of Major A.H.BIBBEY with H.Q./277th A.F.A.Bde. In all, there were 9-18-pdr and 3-4'5" batteries in the Group i.e. all batteries of the 235th, 236th and 277th Brigades. At 5 p.m. the Group co-operated in a CORPS BARRAGE.	
	23rd 24th 26th 27th		Still constituted as above, the LEFT GROUP became the CENTRE GROUP. Following upon preparatory Corps and Army Barrages and Gas Bombardments, the Infantry pursued successful operations, ZERO hour being at 5.50 a.m.this morning. The Divisional Artillery was re-grouped as from 5 p.m, 87th H.Q. being in command of the LEFT GROUP (N IO b 9 4) with "C" and "D" Sub-Groups Commanded respectively by Lt.Col L.SAVILE(H.Q/28th A.F.A.Bde.) and Major A.H.BIBBEY (H.Q/277th A.F.A. Bde.). On the nightz27/28th September the 235th and 236th Brigades withdrew to their Wagon Lines. At 7 p.m. all batteries opened on their S.O.S.Lines and otherwise directed harassing fire against enemy communications.	

Army Form C. 2118.

WAR DIARY
or
INTELLIGENCE SUMMARY
(Erase heading not required.)

Instructions regarding War Diaries and Intelligence Summaries are contained in F. S. Regs., Part II. and the Staff Manual respectively. Title Pages will be prepared in manuscript.

Place	Date	Hour	Summary of Events and Information	Remarks and references to Appendices
			GENERAL	
			From the time Brigade Headquarters moved into action the batteries were generally acting under separate orders, and never under the Brigade Commander for operations save for in the early part of the month when A/87 were included in the CANAL GROUP. All batteries were in action however from 11th September onwards to the end of the month, the No.1 Sub-Group of 22nd – 27th September including "B", "C" and "D"/87 under the command of Major C.H.Tebay B/87, and the later"B" Sub-Group existent from 5 p.m. 27th including all batteries of this Brigade, still commanded by Major C.H.TEBAY. In both cases these Sub-Groups came under the orders of Lt-Col G.S.TOVEY D.S.O. Commanding Right Artillery Group (H.Q./88th F.A.Bde). Prior to this from 11th – 22nd September A/87 were with"B"Sub-Group(Lt.Col. L.SAVILE) and B, C and D/87 with "C" Sub-Group (Lt.Col. CLARKE)H.Q.,/18th A.F.A.Bde. From 22nd – 29th September Lt.Col. L.SAVILE in command of No.2 Sub-Group still had A/87 under his command.	

N.V. Kent

Lieut-Colonel R.F.A.,
Commanding LEFT ARTILLERY GROUP.

CONFIDENTIAL.

19th Division "A".

19th Divisional Artillery.
No B.M. 440.

Herewith War Diary of 19th Divisional Artillery for the month of October 1917.

Please acknowledge receipt.

[signature]

Brigadier-General.
Commanding, 19th Divisional Artillery.

D.A. Headquarters
7th November 1917

WAR DIARY
or
INTELLIGENCE SUMMARY

(Erase heading not required.)

Army Form C. 2118.

Place	Date	Hour	Summary of Events and Information	Remarks and references to Appendices
N.10.b.9.4. (Sheet 28)			**87th F.A.Brigade War Diary – October 1917.**	
	1st		At the beginning of the month the H.Q. of the Bde. was still in action as H.Q. Left Arty.Group, 19th Division. Left Group consisted of "C" and "D" Sub-Groups with H.Q. respectively of 28th and 277th A.F.A.Bdes. Batteries of the Group were heavily shelled, and 65th How: battery especially so. There was much aerial activity both by day and at night, the enemy bombing back areas in the evening.	
	2nd		To-day hostile liveliness in the air was abnormal, 124 Battery position was apparently registered.	
	3rd		Quiet to-day save for the shelling of the 123 Battery area, several casualties resulting:	
	4th 5th		D/87 came into "C" Sub-Group vice 65th How: Bty. transferred to "B" Sub-Group. The Group co-operated in an Army Barrage in the early morning. Subsequent to the operations of the previous day, the Group joined in another barrage to-day. The weather was bad, and this no doubt accounted for the enemy's quietude.	
	1st-6th		During this period Night Firing Programmes on enemy tracks and communications were carried out.	
	6th		During the night bombs were dropped in the battery areas by Hun planes. In a shoot apparently directed by aeroplane, the 124 Battery had five guns put temporarily out of action. At the same time "C"/277, who in common with other batteries of this Brigade had been heavily strafed, had three guns put out of action. In the evening and again in the morning the Group co-operated in Barrages to which the enemy replied quickly but rather weakly.	
	6,7,8th			
	7,8th		This Barrage was repeated on the following night and early morning.	
	8,9th		The inactivity of hostile planes at this juncture was in marked contrast to the liveliness of our own airmen.	
	10-12		On each of these mornings and on the evening of the 12th barrages were put up by our Artillery who also continued their Night Firing Programmes.	
	13,14		To-day a rearrangement of the Divisional Artillery was effected, the Left Group, as now constituted comprising "A" and "D"/87 – "A" & "D"/88 – 123 Bty. & 124 Bty., under the command of Lieut-Colonel W.I.Kent with these Headquarters. The day was quiet generally, but four German balloons were observed, and about 5 p.m. a Boche aviator shot down one of our balloons. In the evening D/88 carried out a gas shoot on ALASKA HOUSES.	

WAR DIARY
or
INTELLIGENCE SUMMARY
(Erase heading not required.)

Place	Date	Hour	Summary of Events and Information	Remarks and references to Appendices
	15th		Early next morning, A/87 were in turn shelled with gas and D/87 and SPOIL BANK received much attention.	
	16th		German machines were very active and on the 17th two of them flew over D/88	
	17th		position flying very low while latterly 3 or 4 flew over the 124 Bty. area. During the day both these positions were heavily shelled as was A/87 in the evening.	
	18th		Again next day A/87 and D/87 were punished - A/87 with gas.	
	19th		Enemy Aeroplanes continued to fly low over battery positions. 123 Battery who had been bombarded the previous evening were again strafed this forenoon. At night D/87 and D/88 joined in a gas shoot on ALASKA HOUSES apart from the usual punishment inflicted on enemy tracks and communications. On the other hand the Hun air machines were again busy bombing.	
	20th		The enemy Artillery displayed great activity. D/87 and 124 batteries being singled out for his especial attention. In the evening his planes bombed 123 Battery position.	
	21st		8 balloons were up this morning and hostile guns were again busy, 2 planes flew low over A/87 position and D/88 and 124 bty were heavily shelled. At 6 p.m. the Divisional Artillery was again reconstituted, Left Group becoming 87th F.A. Brigade with all four batteries of the Brigade under the command of Lieut-Colonel W.J.Kent. "B" and "C"/87 rejoining from the Right Group.	
	22nd		There was a barrage in the morning and the evening was characterised by the usual Programme of Night Firing and by renewed activity on the part of Hun planes. A/87 were heavily shelled this morning.	
	23rd		An Army Barrage was fired at 9-15 a.m. and the enemy reply thereto was weak. Again in the evening harassing fire was directed against the Boche communications lines.	
	25th		To-night and again on the night of the 26th D/87 featured a gas shoot. There was no retaliation of the Divisional front during the operations of the earlier part of to-day.	
	27th		The batteries withdrew to their respective wagon lines, all save A/88 who were relieved by B/88 leaving guards at their Battery positions	
	29th		Headquarters moved to Wagon Lines in LOCRE, and the personnel of the Brigade finished the month in rest.	

W.J.Kent
Lieut-Col.,R.F.A.,
Commanding 87th F.A. Bde.

WAR DIARY
or
INTELLIGENCE SUMMARY

(Erase heading not required.)

Army Form C. 2118.

87 Bde R.F.A Vol 2

Place	Date	Hour	Summary of Events and Information	Remarks and references to Appendices
LOCRE			**87th Brigade R.F.A. November, 1917.**	
	1st-5th		When the month opened the Brigade was in rest, H.Q. being at LOCRE and the Batteries in wagon lines in the Croix de Poperinghe area. On the 3rd the Bde Commander inspected the Bty. Wagon Lines. During the early days of the month a proportion of the Bde. personnel were employed in erecting horse standings in KIM ROAD. To-day the Bde. moved into action relieving 123rd Bde. H.Q. were now at LOCK 7. During the day the Hun planes and Artillery were fairly active, the guns playing especially on roads and railways.	
	5th			
	9th-11th		On the morning of the 5th our own machines were very lively, this in marked contrast to the feature of the late afternoon on the following day. Then, a squadron of 12 E.A. were permitted to fly low over C/87 position without molestation. In the morning of the 8th however 2 Bosche machines were brought down by our own machines. During these days the enemy made an extensive use of his balloons. On the 11th a plane - nationality unknown was brought down near ZANDVOORDE.	
	12th		To-day the enemy indulged in promiscuous area shoots, being especially active with long range - medium calibre guns. In the afternoon a fleet of Gothas flew over our lines.	
	14th		The Bde. moved further left, the batteries relieving those of the 174th F.A. Bde. and H.Q. changing to BEDFORD HOUSE. We now constituted the SOUTHERN ARTILLERY GROUP, acting under orders of the 39th D.A. until the 18th of the month when the 30th D.A. assumed control over the Group. On the 15th the enemy Artillery was active in the vicinity of B/87 gun position and his aircraft were very noticeable in the PASSCHENDAELE area. One of our planes was brought down near GHELUVELT. On the night of the 16th/17th "A" and "C" Batteries were shelled, the latter very heavily. Again, on the 19th C/87 were shelled with 77 mm's, but little material damage, apart from the destruction of the cook-house was occasioned. During the night following B/87 were in turn bombarded. By the 20th each battery had a detached section in action.	
	19/20th			
	22nd		To-day D/87 engaged in a Gas Shoot. On the late afternoon of the 23rd the enemy dropped bombs on ZILLEBEKE	

Place	Date	Hour	Summary of Events and Information	Remarks and references to Appendices
	17/4/30		Throughout this period, night firing programmes of harassing fire were directed against enemy tracks and communications, as also against specially selected targets. On the evening of the 24th the Bde. fired on tracks and buildings in support of Infantry patrols. From the 25th to the 27th GHELUVELT was kept under continual fire, the bombardment in the early evening of the 25th and again in the early morning of the 27th being particularly systematic. On these occasions the portions of GHELUVELT respectively North and South of MENIN ROAD were in turn shelled. Right on until the end of the month GHELUVELT was more or less subjected to continual fire, the system being exemplified by the following bombardment on the morning of the 28th. D/87 then bombarded GHELUVELT for 15 minutes, aided by 5 minute bursts from the 18-pdr batteries. Thereafter A/87 kept GHELUVELT under intermittent fire till noon. In the afternoon a somewhat similar shoot was again carried out by the 4 batteries on dugouts and Shell holes, C/87 on this occasion maintaining the bursts of fire until midnight. M Kent Lieut-Colonel, R.F.A., Commanding Southern Artillery Group.	

Army Form C. 2118.

WAR DIARY
or
INTELLIGENCE SUMMARY.
(Erase heading not required.)

DECEMBER 1917
87th F.A. Bde.
Vol 29

Instructions regarding War Diaries and Intelligence Summaries are contained in F. S. Regs., Part II. and the Staff Manual respectively. Title pages will be prepared in manuscript.

Place	Date	Hour	Summary of Events and Information	Remarks and references to Appendices
BEDFORD HOUSE (nr YPRES)	1st Dec 1917		On the opening day of the month both sides were quiet	
		2nd	At 5.30 am today the 16 bdes cooperated with 9&7 in a bombardment of 5 selected enemy dug outs	
		3rd	At noon the Brigade took part in the barrage incidental to the infantry assault on POLDERHOEK CHATEAU. The enemy retaliated immediately with shrapnel fire on the front of attack.	
		4th	In the morning E.A. were fairly active & in the afternoon our battery positions were bombarded with shells of heavy calibre. Our own artillery in turn fired on enemy working parties	
		5th	Again on the 5th working parties were chopped up by our fire	
		6th	Today, the German guns were exceptionally active, shells of all calibres being expended on battery areas. 9&7 in particular was shelled heavily with 5.9s & 4.2". Also, the aircraft of the enemy carried out extensive reconnaissance flight.	
		7th	So on the the morning of the 7th – marked hostile aerial activity	
		8th	At 11 am on the 8th the 16 F.A bdes batteries assisted 9&7 in a bombardment of a Hun Strongpoint ? Battalion H.Q.	
		9.10th	During the period German artillery became increasingly active. A & C Batteries being heavily shelled on the afternoon of the 10th	
		11th	On the 12th however, the Boche was unusually quiet though a fleet of Bohas flew over the Bty positions in the morning & again in the early afternoon.	

Army Form C. 2118.

WAR DIARY
or
INTELLIGENCE SUMMARY.
(Erase heading not required.)

Instructions regarding War Diaries and Intelligence Summaries are contained in F.S. Regs., Part II. and the Staff Manual respectively. Title pages will be prepared in manuscript.

Place	Date	Hour	Summary of Events and Information	Remarks and references to Appendices
	13th		D/87 fired on dugouts & X roads at 6 a.m. assisted by the 16-pdr Batteries on the 14th. C/91 carried out a shoot on observed target.	
	15/16th		Enemy artillery was quiet, but his planes showed considerable activity in morning of the 16th.	
	17th		Today much hostile movement was observed in the vicinity of QUART BUILDINGS.	
	18/19th		During the night A & D Batteries were heavily shelled but by daytime on the 19th the German guns were quiet. Later on in the evening, however, they subjected our batteries to a very vigorous gas bombardment.	
	21st		Major Newbery M.C. assumed command of the Brigade, still known as Southern Group, during the temporary absence of Lt.Col Kent on leave.	
	23rd		In the early morning there was heavy enemy shelling of all Batteries: in the afternoon one of our scouts pursued a Hun plane & ultimately the latter crashed to earth. Still later, at 6.30 p.m. D/67 bombarded HAMP FARM & a suspected T.M. Emplacement - all 18pdr batteries cooperating.	
	1st - 23rd		Throughout the whole period, a systematic programme of night firing was carried out on special selected Tasks comprising roads, tracks & strong points	

WAR DIARY
or
INTELLIGENCE SUMMARY

(Erase heading not required.)

Army Form C. 2118.

Place	Date	Hour	Summary of Events and Information	Remarks and references to Appendices
	24/25		During this period nothing of special importance took place, as during the day-time observation was impossible owing to fog. At night, the usual night firing programme was carried out on special selected tasks.	
	26		Today, some movement was observed along track T28b.60.22 to QUART BUILDINGS. the Battrie being disturbed by a few rounds being fired on this spot by C/87.	
	27		On this day, the Brigade came out of action, being relieved by the 242 A.F.A Brigade. Each battery moved from the scene of action to its respective wagon Lines, while the Head Quarters moved from BEDFORD HOUSE to ST JANS CAPPEL.	
	28		This day went nothing of importance, the time being spent chiefly in preparation for a further move.	
	29/30		Today, the Brigade moved from their respective wagon Lines and journeyed to BAILLEUL. At this town entraining operations were carried out, and during the next day (30th) the different batteries, together with Head quarters, arrived at BAPAUME. From this station, at different intervals throughout	

WAR DIARY
INTELLIGENCE SUMMARY.
(Erase heading not required.)

Army Form C. 2118.

Place	Date	Hour	Summary of Events and Information	Remarks and references to Appendices
	31st		The day and night, each unit of the Brigade proceeded to the camp at ROCQUIGNY, where a halt was made till the next morning. The last day of the year, and made the 1st December, came with movement for the Brigade during the morning. The camp at ROCQUIGNY was quitted and a journey made to ETRICOURT, by way of BOS-YTRES and the BEET-ROOT FACTORY. Although the roads were frost-bound and very slippery in places, yet the journey was carried out successfully.	

Hollenby
Major R.F.A.
Comdg. 87 = F.A. Bde

WAR DIARY
or
INTELLIGENCE SUMMARY

Army Form C. 2118.

67 Bde RFA Vol 30

87th BRIGADE RFA – JANUARY 1918.

Place	Date	Hour	Summary of Events and Information	Remarks and references to Appendices
ETRICOURT	1st	–	The first day of the New Year was spent in ETRICOURT but on the morning of the 2nd preparations were begun for the return of the Brigade into action. The Wagon lines moved to NEUVILLE.	
	2nd	–	Batteries going into action to the relief of the 78th Brigade units	
NEUVILLE	3rd	–	The Whole Brigade now moved into action. HQ controlling 15 CENTRE Group comprising 106 Brigade Batteries together with B and D/55. 987 were bombed on the METZ-TRESCAULT Road, and they moved into action.	
	4th		Quiet. From the commencement of a Night Firing Programme on roads & trenches this day was eventless	
	5th		Today, there was a marked increase in the aerial activity shown by both sides, and by night the usual programme was carried through	
	6th		Considerable movement was reported on the SUNKEN ROAD between NINE WOOD & MARCOING. This was engaged with good effect. Also 867 shorts the silencing of a Machine Gun which had been located at L.28.6.55 (Sheet 57C NE)	
	7th		Eventless	
	8th		At 9am today the Grouping of the Divisional Artillery was reorganised. B+ B/55 teamed to the Command of the Left Group together with I.B.7, while H.Q. of this Brigade now became HQ RIGHT HEADQUARTERS GROUP, constituted as follows:— B.C+D/67, 6 C/55 and all Batteries of the	

Army Form C. 2118.

WAR DIARY
or
INTELLIGENCE SUMMARY.
(Erase heading not required.)

Place	Date	Hour	Summary of Events and Information	Remarks and references to Appendices
HINDENBURG SUPPORT	8th	-	298th FA Brigade as the Right Sub-Group.	
	9th	-	A systematic programme of Night firing was directed against enemy communications & strong points. In the early morning HQ Wagon Line was bombed, 7 HD being killed & 11 men, including 2/Lt Brown wounded.	
	10th	-	Today the German fire on the vicinity of BEAUCHAMP was particularly heavy. The aerial activity manifested by both sides was also above normal.	
	11th	-	HQ. of the Right Sub-Group ceased to exist as such. The units comprising it coming under the direct control of these HQ. On the 13th however, HQ. 298 & 70 Brigade relieved HQ 187, who then withdrew to the Wagon Lines at NEUVILLE BOURJONVAL.	
	13th			
	14th-21st	-	Throughout this week, HQ remained at rest in NEUVILLE, the Batteries remaining under the Right and Left Groups for tactical purposes.	
	22nd	-	HQ again moved into action as controlling unit of the Right Group. The Batteries now under the command of Lt-Col Kent comprised B, C & D/67 with A & D/77.	
	23rd	-	Very unexpected & embarrassing were the casualties sustained by HQ on this date, no fewer than 21 members of the Staff being admitted to Hospital as gas patients. Prompt action was taken however to have the vacancies suitably filled.	
	23rd/24th	-	During the night 7 Group Batteries engaged several roads within the Enemy's lines.	

Army Form C. 2118.

WAR DIARY
or
INTELLIGENCE SUMMARY.
(Erase heading not required.)

Instructions regarding War Diaries and Intelligence Summaries are contained in F. S. Regs., Part II. and the Staff Manual respectively. Title pages will be prepared in manuscript.

Place	Date	Hour	Summary of Events and Information	Remarks and references to Appendices
	24/1	-	C/87 and D/77 engaged & disposed German working parties by night. The usual harassing fire was carried out on enemy roads & communications. Aircraft were active throughout the day in forward areas	
	25/1	-	Today batteries of the Group again fired on hostile working parties, strong points, roads & centres of movement in general. The enemy artillery was also active shelling Bose Coise very heavily from 5 to 6.30 p.m. Some of the firing was done on aerial observation, two balloons & 7 aeroplanes being able to be browned.	
	26/1	-	The Boche was quieter today but our own firing was on the customary lines	
	28/1	-	D/77 today responded to an NF call for being directed on crossroads and on the enemy lines. C/87 on the other hand, fired in response to the liaison officer's call & again in the evening with the Silsburg Guns. This later method of offensive was featured in the nightly programme. 18 pdr batteries of the Group manning the gun in turn. Some enemy movement was observed.	
	29/1		Enemy artillery very active on battery areas during the day and night. It is early morning of the 30th. The vicinity of HQ was subjected to a heavy gas shell bombardment later in the forenoon, movement was engaged by our batteries and good effect & subsequently	
	30/1			

T2134. Wt. W708—775. 500000. 4/15. Sir J. C. & S.

Army Form C. 2118.

WAR DIARY
or
INTELLIGENCE SUMMARY.
(Erase heading not required.)

Place	Date	Hour	Summary of Events and Information	Remarks and references to Appendices
	30th	—	The usual night firing and searching gun programmes were carried out. The about a feature of the day's work was raid by our airmen who forced 6 German balloons to descend, two of these being hit. One of the enemy aviators on the other had observed for one of his batteries. The efforts of our anti-aircraft guns to drive him off being quite in vain	
	31st	—	The C.O. of the Brigade today inspected the various wagon lines the while the C.O. R.A. paid a visit to the Battery positions	

W. Kent.
Lieut- Col R.F.A.
Comdg. 87th F.A. Brigade.

WAR DIARY
or
INTELLIGENCE SUMMARY
(Erase heading not required.)

Army Form C. 2118.

87 Bde RFA Vol 31

Place	Date	Hour	Summary of Events and Information	Remarks and references to Appendices
Q12 a 25 (Sheet 51C) 1/20,000			**87TH BRIGADE RFA – FEBRUARY 1918**	
	1st		At the beginning of the month Headquarters of the Brigade still controlled the Right Artillery Group, comprising B, C & D Batteries of the Brigade together with A and D/177 A/67, and the Lahore Section of February acted under the command of 14th A.G. Artillery Group.	
	1st-3rd		During this period the customary bombardments & night firing were directed against enemy strongpoints and communications. By day movement within the German lines was repeatedly engaged, and in the evening enemy contacted to be featured.	
	4th		Today retaliation was given by the Group to a hostile Trench & Mortar bombardment. Also, one section of each of the 77th Brigade batteries was relieved by units of the 223rd F.A. Brigade (63rd Royal Naval Division) Night firing was carried out as usual.	
	5th		The relief begun on the 4th was now completed, C and D/223 now being in action in units of the Group to the exclusion of A and D/177.	
	6th	4.30 am	In the early morning Batteries of the Group carried out "Counter-Preparation" fire.	
	7th	1.15am	At this hour the S.O.S. call was received from the 4th A/Tk Bn as the enemy infantry in a 47th battalion on the line Aircraft reported weapons. During the day enemy movement was engaged on several occasions; the vicinity of D/17 in particular being searched heavily shelled with 4.2s and 5.9s. Our artillery carried out a programme of H.V. firing on to usual lines.	

G.O.C. R.A. inspected Wagon Lines

Army Form C. 2118.

Instructions regarding War Diaries and Intelligence Summaries are contained in F.S. Regs., Part II. and the Staff Manual respectively. Title pages will be prepared in manuscript.

WAR DIARY
or
INTELLIGENCE SUMMARY.
(Erase heading not required.)

Place	Date	Hour	Summary of Events and Information	Remarks and references to Appendices
	8/4		Enemy movement engaged at various times during the day. The usual programme of night firing and sniping was carried out by batteries of the Group. In the evening C/87 sustained 7 casualties the while a gun was being brought into a new position.	
	9/4		The Group today engaged principally an enemy cutting. The effects being observed as very good. Enemy movement was also disposed of and various strong points within his lines were shelled. D/87 in particular engaged a Trench Mortar with good effect. By counter enemy artillery was quiet.	
	10/4		In the late afternoon of today C/87 position & vicinity was shelled with 300 rds 4.2s and 5.9s. Remaining guns & pits were destroyed & one officer (2nd Lt L. Batson) wounded. C/223 were also bombarded in the course of the day.	
	11/4		Usual programme of firing by day and night with a special night shoot on enemy centres of movement.	
	12/4		Quiet but in the later hours of the night and again in the early morning C/223 were bombarded with 4.2s. Little damage being done.	
	13/4		Normal activity on either side.	
	14/4		Cessation of each. C/87 was relieved in action by sections of batteries of the 123rd A.F.A. Bde.	
	15/4		On the following day the relief of all batteries was completed H.Q. was withdrawn to the Dragoon Lines at NEUVILLE BOURJONVAL, C/87 being located on the same village. The horse manning of wagon lines were situated in TREES.	

2353 Wt. W3544/1454 700,000 5/15 D.D.&L. A.D.S.S./Forms/C.2118.

Army Form C. 2118.

WAR DIARY
or
INTELLIGENCE SUMMARY.
(Erase heading not required.)

Instructions regarding War Diaries and Intelligence Summaries are contained in F. S. Regs., Part II. and the Staff Manual respectively. Title pages will be prepared in manuscript.

Place	Date	Hour	Summary of Events and Information	Remarks and references to Appendices
NEUVILLE s FOSSES	16th -19th	-	General cleaning up & training	
	20th		The Brigade Commander inspected all wagon lines today	
	21st-25th		Ordinary Brigade routine	
	25th	-	Today Lt. Col. C.R. Peel CMG DSO assumed command of the Brigade vice Lt Col W.F. Reid admitted to Hospital 9/2/18	
	26th		Tactical scheme carried out by Brigade	
	27th		Tactical scheme was carried out by HQ and all Batteries in cooperation with other Divisional units.	
	28th		HQ. A and B Batteries carried out a scheme	

28/2/18

W.R. Peel
Lieut-Col RA
Comdg 87th Brigade RFA

19th Divisional Artillery.

WAR DIARY

This Diary is partly mutilated.

87th BRIGADE

ROYAL FIELD ARTILLERY

MARCH 1918

Army Form C. 2118.

87 Bde R.F.A.

WAR DIARY
or
INTELLIGENCE SUMMARY.
(Erase heading not required.)

87th Brigade R.F.A. – March 1918

Place	Date	Hour	Summary of Events and Information	Remarks and references to Appendices
NEUVILLE BOURJONVAL	1st–3rd 3rd/4th 4/21st		Ordinary Brigade routine in Wagon lines at NEUVILLE BOURJONVAL & YPRES Batteries relieved units of 235 F.A. Bde in action near TRESCAULT, Wagons remaining at rest. Ordinary Brigade routine at Wagon lines. In action, the Batteries experienced some time notably from 11th to 13th when they were subjected to intense gas shell bombardments. B & D/87 were particularly heavily shelled.	
	21st		Early in the morning, the enemy delivered a very violent and prolonged preliminary bombardment. Back areas & villages received considerable attention during this period.	
	22nd		Headquarters, in chief since early morning took up a forward position between NEUVILLE and METZ in the afternoon, but subsequently withdrew in the evening to the original HQ in NEUVILLE. With the enemy pushing forward vigorously, the Brigade was withdrawn in the afternoon to positions on the LE MESNIL Road later in the evening, the Brigade withdrew still further to positions near LE TRANSLOY (UI9 BOCQUIGNY)	
LE MESNIL	23rd			
LE SARS	24th		In the morning the Germans continued to attack & Batteries & HQ retired gradually to the vicinity of LE SARS. the batteries being in action there in the evening with HQ near COURCELETTE Next day, the entire Brigade moved along the COURCELETTE–POZIERES Road. the batteries fighting with easy reach of POZIERES & again near LA BOISELLE In the evening HQ. drew across the ridge to AVELUY. Batteries following later.	
POZIERES –AVELUY	25th 26th			
MARTINSART	27th		Next morning, a further retirement was made on MARTINSART. HQ. remaining in the village while the Batteries took up positions on the ridge behind. there the Brigade remained until relief in the late afternoon of the 27th Headed by HQ the Bde	
MARIEUX –DOMART	27th 28th		Thence on the 28th until H.Q. ... to have a halt was made ...ed to MARIEUX	87 F. Bde.

19th Divisional Artillery.

87th BRIGADE R. F. A.   APRIL 1918.

WAR DIARY or INTELLIGENCE SUMMARY

87 Bir R... 101

87th Brigade HQ - April 1918

Place	Date	Hour	Summary of Events and Information	Remarks and references to Appendices
	1st		The Brigade marched from COUCHY & continued on proceeding via STR. & CALONNE to RADINGHEM along the road was attacked again by the enemy & after a stiff fight, proceeded again to join a more or less made this armistice action in the O.W. 2nd & 3rd The Brigade rallied & made a stand on the VIEUX BERQUIN - OUTERSTEENE - STEENWERCK & NEUVE EGLISE road. MESSINES Sector. HQ finally being attached to 9th Bn. of the WARNETON - MESSINES road.	
	3rd/4th		The 87th Bde Group comprising all Infantry of the Bgde still in action A/67 Bn guides the 87th in attack & capturing the Bn lines. The front was quiet during the period hostile artillery displaying no activity. A new artillery line on the old hard cavalry and tramways of light tramways of enemy raids or attacks were on the offensive to 8th the brigade's portion of the troops collapsed and it. Wounded a Shell artillery. Lewis Machine emplacement.	
	10th		Following up the attack of the previous day on the Dismantlings front to the German today turned an attack against the Scherpenberg. Sir Wrights Composite was ousted to Red Barn to help 183rd 87th entered the Red Barn & Lt Col. Part 1. Lt Col. Part 1 Suvla as C.O. Div taking command J.J.T.O. took over Battalion. HQ continued to hostilities in vicinity of Bieghem Belgian.	
	11th/12th/13th		Battalions remained the army but HQ was every establish in the... attack of German Hun attacks. In the early morning of the 13th B.G. moved to the new site of Battery in the early morning of the 13th a first the situation was made to Fairy Porch battalion taking up positions in the vicinity.	
	15th			
	16th		On the 16th HQ again moved and the Infantry Bde HQ along these been maintained to SCHERPENBERG Hill, but on the following day, HQ departed to 200 yds to the neighbourhood. LOBBES - La CUTTE Road. Lieut Croft now became Campbell's Grand Major.	

Having assumed command on the 11th of Lt Col Part.

WAR DIARY
or
INTELLIGENCE SUMMARY.
(Erase heading not required.)

Army Form C. 2118.

Place	Date	Hour	Summary of Events and Information	Remarks and references to Appendices
19¹	19¹		About this period the Corps were covering the retiring of the 28th French Division, division of M Carnassa's Group being established with Messimy's Artillery Group. From now until the 23rd the enemy was comparatively quiet he while our guns remained active on enemy roads & approaches	
	23rd/24th		German artillery was very violent during the evening of the 23rd and again the 24th. Now the Bars, the French recaptured Daylight's Corner & Donegal Farm on the evening of the 24th	
	25th		Commencing about 2.30 a.m. the Germans opened a most intense bombardment, & lately advanced Batteries were compelled to withdraw after had to load engagements more a Lieut. 7. A.C. & D/67 together with B/68. Lost heavily engaging the remaining of Batteries were now promoted into Major Russell's Command & withdrawn in the late afternoon to positions beyond OUDERDOM. H.Q. until the remaining of Batteries A.C.1 D/68 & B/67 again moved forward to positions near RENINGHELST. German artillery were comparatively inactive	
	26th		The Brigade gave cribume fire action to wagon lines beyond HERELE. Next day was shout there but on the 29th the entire 81st Brigade marched under Major to Selle Croix, the route followed being STEENVOORDE - CAESTRE - BRANCHOVE - PECQUINGHEM for the Brigade went into rest	
	27th			

signature
T. Major 67A.
Commanding 67th Brigade 7A.

87 Bde RFA
Vol 34

WAR DIARY or INTELLIGENCE SUMMARY

Army Form C. 2118.

Place	Date	Hour	Summary of Events and Information	Remarks and references to Appendices

87th Brigade R.F.A. - May 1918

Belle Croix	12-17		During this period the Brigade was at rest in the vicinity of Belle Croix. Inspections were carried out on the 15th & 17th inst. by the G.O.C. R.A. 2nd Army & the G.O.C. XV Corps respectively.	
Le Bizerou	17th		The Brigade now moved to lines near Le Bizerou. The Ordnance Brigade routine was relieved by the fitting of stores. On 16th May the G.O.C. inspected the Brigade in Field Service Marching Order.	
	18th		Today the Brigade entrained at Somer and Reques & proceeded via Etaples - Noyelles sur Mer - St Denis - Chateau Thierry - Epernay to detraining stations of Chalons & Vitry la Ville.	
Dampierre-sur-Moivre	19th		Thence, the march was continued to Dampierre-sur-Moivre where the entire Brigade entered training billets.	
	20th 27th		Ordinary Brigade routine	
Bisseuil	28th		Today the Brigade marched via Longevas - Stribienne - Chalons - Juvigny - Toies-sur-Marne to Bisseuil.	
Saucy	29th		March continued via Av - Comieres - Houtvilleres - Nanteuil - Morieux - Chaumuzy - Sarcy Brigade HQ remained in the distained village while the Batteries went into action in front of the village.	
Chaumuzy	30th 31st		Batteries & HQ were compelled today to withdraw to positions in round & in Chaumuzy from these positions they continued to resist the German advance.	

W.J. Sturgeon
Major R.F.A.
Commanding 87th Brigade R.F.A.

87 Bde R F
Vol 35

Army Form C. 2118.

WAR DIARY
or
INTELLIGENCE SUMMARY.
(Erase heading not required.)

Place	Date	Hour	Summary of Events and Information	Remarks and references to Appendices
CHAUMUZY	1st		87th Brigade 1st – 7th June 1918. For the greater part of the day the Brigade was still occupying positions around CHAUMUZY assisted in holding up the German advance. In the evening however, the batteries fell back on position in front of MAREUIL with HQrs in a small wood S.E. of BULLIN.	
	2nd-5th		During the greater part of this period there was but little hostile artillery activity. Our guns on the other hand carried out systematic shoots on enemy valleys, roads, tracks & enemy movement in general. About 2.55am on 6th June the Germans opened a heavy bombardment of MAREUIL & vicinity with gas and HE, the shelling lasting until 5am, extent in the end, reducing any material gain temporary German successes in the Bureau of front were latterly neutralised by spirited counter-attack. Hostile-ply so in the region of MONT BLIGNY. In the evening in consequence Batteries still remained in their original positions although HQ had moved a new into the BOIS de COURTON.	
	7th		Generally, the next three days were quiet enough, our own programmes of harassing fire corresponding to German programmes which earned particularly for the MAREUIL district all the Bois des Eclisses. From 3 to 6 am on the 9th the enemy bombarded the battery areas with shells of all calibres from 77mm to 10.5cm. gas being employed as well as HE, but there again no enemy action of consequence ensued.	
	10/13th		Broadly, the activity of hostile artillery may be summarised as normal, the artillery on either hand shooting on lines that have been already indicated. Standing out prominently possibly, was the abnormal aerial activity between 5 & 8 p.m on the 12th, and as our bombs of exploration fire on the evening of the 14th. On the 16th to Brigade released by an Italian and withdrew from action on 18th June, the next was just Wagon Lines was established temporarily about a mile North of HAUTEVILLERS. But on 19th moving to 20th, the Brigade, in common with the whole of the Divisional Artillery, marched South via EPERNAY to VERTUS area.	
HAUTEVILLERS VERTUS.	19th 20th			

Place	Date	Hour	Summary of Events and Information	Remarks and references to Appendices
	21st		On the morning the march was continued to BARNES, and here the Brigade remained until the last day of the month. The period generally was devoted to training, and battery tests for gun layers were carried out, but great attention was also paid to recreation and the Brigade Sports together with the inter-battery football cup proved to be outstanding successes. On the last day of June, "A" and "B" Batteries marched to entraining stations respectively at FERE-en-CHAMPENOISE & SOMMESOUS: the remaining batteries following up on 1st July.	

W M Stewart
Lieut-Col R.G.A.
Comdg 87th Brigade R.G.A.

WAR DIARY
or
INTELLIGENCE SUMMARY
(Erase heading not required.)

Army Form C. 2118.

87 Bde R.F.A

Vol 36

Place	Date	Hour	Summary of Events and Information	Remarks and references to Appendices
			87th Brigade R.F.A – July 1918.	
THIENBRONNE	1st to 2nd	3rd to 12th	In the early morning the Brigade entrained at FERE-en-TARDENOIS & journeyed via the outskirts of PARIS & ETAPLES to MARQUISE. Thence units marched independently via HESDIN, FRUGES & FAUQUEMBERGUES to THIENBRONNE.	
			This was a training period. Section and Battery gun drill, laying & range setting, signalling, setting up drill's laying & firing being emphasised. Tactical schemes were carried out. Including Shell one minute. B/Battery Staff Parades.	
ERNY ST JULIEN	13th	13th to 31st	The Brigade moved today to the Fifth Army Training Area. H.Q.rs and batteries were now billeted in ERNY-ST-JULIEN.	
			Further training programmes were now carried out on a progressive basis. Lectures on such subjects as Light Testing, Director Calibration, Long Range Shooting & Ranging being featured throughout. Similarly classes were held for instructors in Lewis Guns & Musketry. The general scheme of training emphasised Section & Bty Training, Gun Drill, Laying & Signalling etc. as at THIENBRONNE. Tactical schemes were again carried out, that on 27th July being undertaken in conjunction with Infantry & Heavy Artillery. Batteries also carried out shooting practice on the range at WESTRETIEN, and on 23rd inst. all guns & Hows, were calibrated at TILQUES.	

W R Reid
Lt Col R.F.A.
Comg 87th Brigade R.F.A

WAR DIARY
or
INTELLIGENCE SUMMARY.
(Erase heading not required.)

Army Form C. 2118.

Place	Date	Hour	Summary of Events and Information	Remarks and references to Appendices
			8th Brigade R.F.A – August 1918	
ERNY-ST-JULIEN	1st/5th	–	Brigade still in training area – Carrying out gas-setting gundrill etc	
LAPUGNOY	6th	–	1918. Today marched via ESTREE BLANCHE, FERFAY, AUCHEL by the MINES area the Brigade being billeted for the night at & around LAPUGNOY. Sections of each battery proceeded straight away into action	
BETHUNE	7th		The Brigade now relieved the 147/FA Bde in the line FO & batteries occupying positions near BETHUNE.	147-B-N.E. 4
	Period		In the period from now until the close of the month was a quiet one marked by more activity on our own part than on that of the enemy. The beginning of the period and upon towards the end of August the Germans gradually withdrawing on our front. But at no time was his artillery really active & only on two or three nights were his bombing planes active. Our batteries, on the other hand, carried out nightly programmes of sniping on enemy roads tracks & bridges about known enemy in special shoots. Many gun was also provided throughout by the Brigade and in the latter days of the month single forward guns were employed in harassing the enemy and could readily following subaltern officers in reconnaissance observation etc	3½-S.E. 1/20,000 BETHUNE 4" one
	12th 18th		On the night of the 12/13th the Brigade – known as the "Right Group" carried a raid by our infantry. Today a destructive shoot was undertaken on selected targets, houses etc in conjunction with the howers.	
	24th		Assistance was given to the 40th DA in their bombardment today of the LACOUTURE area. The 47th Bde now came under the order of the 1st Corps Light Sub Group	
	26th		Today a regrouping of the Artillery left the "Light Group" consisted of all batteries F.Q.B. 147 & 347 Bde & 347 with their H.Q. situated as before	

16

WR 37

Army Form C. 2118.

WAR DIARY
or
INTELLIGENCE SUMMARY.
(Erase heading not required.)

Instructions regarding War Diaries and Intelligence Summaries are contained in F. S. Regs., Part II. and the Staff Manual respectively. Title pages will be prepared in manuscript.

Place	Date	Hour	Summary of Events and Information	Remarks and references to Appendices
BETHUNE	28		On the night 28/29th Light Sgt Essars Artillery Groups put up a barrage in support of an attack by the Infantry. The attack was unsuccessful.	
	29		D/177 was passed to the control of the Lt A Artillery Group. In the late evening D/177 B/41 moved to forward positions.	
	30/31		Now advanced the battery position × 2 A.9.9.	

Lt/Col
Cmdg 2/A 177 E.F.A.
France

WAR DIARY
INTELLIGENCE SUMMARY

87 Bde R.F.A.

Place	Date	Hour	Summary of Events and Information	Remarks and references to Appendices
			87th BRIGADE R.F.A. - SEPTEMBER 1918.	
LOCON	1st	-	Today H.Q. moved from the Canal Bank near BETHUNE to a forward position at X.1 & 2 near LOCON. All Batteries of the group less A guns of A/87 but including C/87 Battery were now located around VIEILLE CHAPELLE. Lt.Col. Peel still being in command of the Right Group.	2 Maps 36.A S.E.
	2nd		The remaining sections of A/87 now came into line & all batteries carried out registration.	
	3rd		At 5.30 am today the Artillery of the Division opened in support of an Infantry attack unsuccessful our troops advancing beyond the LA BASSEE ROAD.	
	4th		In the early morning H.B Batteries of the Engagement gas shelled. But later the whole troops again took in cooperation with an attack by the Division on the night time again all objectives were gained.	
	6th		Still acting as Right Group H.Q. to controlling centre was now changed to X 26 a 7. near LOISNE CHATEAU Right Group Brofer now comprised B & C/146 with E & D/87: & Left Group HO & 146 & Z.A. Brigade. Sheet 96 A S.E.	
LOISNE			being composed of A - B/87 and A & B/146	
			On the Front the enemy guns were inactive	
	7th		The Left & Right assisted in a successful operation by the Left Brigade of the Division	
	10th		D/87 today undertook a signal gun cutting shoot	
	11th		The Night Firing programme throughout the period was in the nature of harassing fire, enemy strong points & centres of movement	
	13th		C/146 now withdrew from action, the control & direction group was reassigned by the 7. F. Hamick of A/87 Lt.Col. Peel having taken over, command of the 19/DA On the 13th Lousie Major Hamick was relieved by Lt.Col. F.B. Riddle of the 146 Brigade and 16 Group was no commended	
16/17th			until the withdrawal of the 146 F.A. Brigade on the nights 16 & 17th September	

Army Form C. 2118.

WAR DIARY
or
INTELLIGENCE SUMMARY.
(Erase heading not required.)

Place	Date	Hour	Summary of Events and Information	Remarks and references to Appendices
LOISNE	16th 17th		Prior to this the Left Sub Group had cooperated in a minor infantry operation on the morning of the 16th. With the outgoing of the 46th Brigade, the 19th Divisional Artillery were reinforced by the 179th A.F.A. Brigade. The 383, 463 & 464 Batteries were attached to the Left Group, command of which had now passed to Lt.Col. J.C. Fulleston until now Commander of 267. The erstwhile Brigade Commander Lt.Colonel E.T.R. Peel now became Brig-Gen Comdg 19th D.A.	
	21st		Today the cooperation of the entire Group was lent to an attack by the Infantry, the object of which embraced the capture of SHEPHERD'S REDOUBT, the DISTILLERY & YORK TRENCH. All objectives were gained but the enemy had occupied by 23rd and in rebuilding all these strongholds.	
	23rd 25th		On the 23rd the hostile artillery was particularly active. Starting at 6 am a second attack was launched with objectives similar to that of the 21st. Our Artillery firing a barrage in support. The assault was completely successful & all	
	28th		ground held against enemy counter attacks. The Group, less 383 Bty which had now joined the Left Artillery Group commanded by Lt Col Walrond with HQ at 188 R.F.A. Bde. joined in a general 5th Army programme of harassing fire. Night enemy programmes were carried out throughout the month on the usual lines enemy roads, tracks, billets, bivouacs strongholds receiving special attention.	
	29th 30th		The concentrations of the 28th were foggy and repeated. Concentrations again carried out. The Group cooperated in an operation undertaken by the Left Brigade	179 A.F.A. Lieut Col R.F.A. Comdg 87th Brigade R.F.A.

H.Q.
82nd Bde...

Date. 30/9/18

Army Form C. 2118.

WAR DIARY
or
INTELLIGENCE SUMMARY.
(Erase heading not required)

Instructions regarding War Diaries and Intelligence Summaries are contained in F. S. Regs., Part II. and the Staff Manual respectively. Title pages will be prepared in manuscript.

67th BRIGADE R.F.A.
October 1918.

Place	Date	Hour	Summary of Events and Information	Remarks and references to Appendices
LOISNE	1st		At the beginning of the month Headquarters were still at LOISNE, all batteries of the Brigade together with 463 & 464 Batteries being in action under the command of Lt-Col. Fullerton.	
	2nd.		Early in the morning it became apparent that the enemy was withdrawing in the Divisional sector and sections of "A" & "B" Batteries were sent forward to cover the advance of our infantry.	
LIGNY le GRAND	3rd		All Batteries now moved forward, and Headquarters were established in LIGNY le GRAND; 463 & 464 Batteries now went into close reserve.	
			On the 4th there were no changes in the dispositions of the Brigade.	
HERLIES	5th		Headquarters today moved to HERLIES, and Battery positions were occupied in the vicinity of WICRES	
	6th. to 8th.		Throughout this period, the German Artillery displayed marked activity, especially on FOURNES; the fire of our own batteries was rather modified.	
	10th		D/87 co-operated at 05.15 in a raid covered for the most part by the Left Artillery Group.	
	11th		463 & 464 Batteries now moved into action	
	12th		464 Battery fired in support of a midnight Infantry raid on a Hun Post.	
	13th.		Eventless.	
	14th.		A/87 & B/87, relieved in action by units of the 44th A.F.A. Brigade, retired to Wagon Lines in the neighbourhood of ESSARS.	
	15th.		The relief of the Brigade was now completed, and both "C" & "D" Batteries moved to Wagon Lines adjoining those of the other Batteries, but Headquarters remained in the "action" billets until the following day, when the entire Headquarters moved to BETHUNE.	
BETHUNE	16th			
	17th.		Starting with H.Q., who entrained at midday, the whole Brigade entrained at BETHUNE for BAPAUME.	
CAMBRAI	18th.		On arrival at BAPAUME, all units of the Brigade marched independently to CAMBRAI, billets for all being obtained temporarily in the town.	
AVESNES les AUBERT	19th.		On the evening of the 19th, however, a further march was begun, and by noon on the 20th, all units were established in AVESNES les AUBERT. Here the Brigade remained until the 21st inst.	
HAUSSY	21st.		The Brigade then moved into action, with HQ. in HAUSSY, and the Batteries in position in the neighbourhood of the village.	
	22nd.		Registration was carried out by all Batteries.	
	23rd.		Batteries silent.	
	24th.		The Brigade co-operated this morning in an attack by the 61st Division, which was carried out	

Army Form C. 2118.

WAR DIARY
or
INTELLIGENCE SUMMARY.

(Erase heading not required.)

Place	Date	Hour	Summary of Events and Information	Remarks and references to Appendices
St.Martin	25th		In conjunction with attacks delivered by the 6th & 22nd Corps. Zero hour was at 04.00 hours. Subsequent to the successful operations of the preceding day, Headquarters now moved to a forward position on the outskirts of ST MARTIN. Batteries took up positions in the vicinity, but for the time, the whole Brigade was merely in close reserve. Until the 28th October all was quiet, although the German Artillery was fairly active on ST MARTIN and environs.	
	28th		On the 28th fresh Battery positions were reconnoitred in squares Q 17 & Q 18 (reference sheet France 51 a.)	
	29th 30th 31st		During the 29th the guns were carefully registered. Batteries remained silent during the following day. These new positions were now fully manned, together with an advanced Headquarters at Q 16 c 2 1.	

1.11.18

[signature]
Lieut-Colonel R.F.A.
Commanding 87th Brigade R.F.A.

www.ingramcontent.com/pod-product-compliance
Lightning Source LLC
Chambersburg PA
CBHW081359160426
43193CB00013B/2067